MILLENNIAL
NUNS

MILLENNIAL NUNS

REFLECTIONS
on LIVING *a*
SPIRITUAL LIFE
in a WORLD *of*
SOCIAL MEDIA

THE DAUGHTERS *of* SAINT PAUL

SIMON ELEMENT

NEW YORK   LONDON   TORONTO   SYDNEY   NEW DELHI

SIMON ELEMENT

An Imprint of Simon & Schuster, Inc.
1230 Avenue of the Americas
New York, NY 10020

First Simon Element trade paperback edition July 2022

SIMON ELEMENT is a trademark of Simon & Schuster, Inc.

For information about special discounts for bulk purchases, please contact Simon & Schuster Special Sales at 1-866-506-1949 or business@simonandschuster.com.

The Simon & Schuster Speakers Bureau can bring authors to your live event. For more information or to book an event, contact the Simon & Schuster Speakers Bureau at 1-866-248-3049 or visit our website at www.simonspeakers.com.

Interior design by Laura Levatino

1 3 5 7 9 10 8 6 4 2

Library of Congress Cataloging-in-Publication Data

Names: Daughters of St. Paul, author.
Title: Millennial nuns: inspiring words for women on how to live and lead with courage, confidence, and authenticity / by The Daughters of Saint Paul.
Description: New York : Tiller Press, 2021. |
Identifiers: LCCN 2020049734 (print) | LCCN 2020049735 (ebook) |
ISBN 9781982158026 | ISBN 9781982158040 (ebook)
Subjects: LCSH: Christian life—Catholic authors. | Nuns.
Classification: LCC BX2350.3 .D38 2021 (print) | LCC BX2350.3 (ebook) |
DDC 248.4/82—dc23
LC record available at https://lccn.loc.gov/2020049734
LC ebook record available at https://lccn.loc.gov/2020049735

ISBN 978-1-9821-5803-3
ISBN 978-1-9821-5804-0 (ebook)

*To all the Daughters of Saint Paul who have gone before us,
those with us . . . and all those who will come after us*

CONTENTS

CONTENTS

MILLENNIAL
NUNS

FOREWORD

Sr. Marie James Hunt, FSP

I am honored to present to you this book about the #MillennialNuns of the Daughters of Saint Paul. It is part memoir, part inspirational guide, showing how our sisters balance both being millennials and Catholic religious sisters. First, a couple of disclaimers: we Daughters of St. Paul are technically not nuns. The differences between a religious sister and a religious nun are that we sisters are engaged in society, sharing our lives, prayer, and ministry externally, while a religious nun remains in her cloister offering prayers and sacrifices such as silence and fasting as her main ministry. The commonalities between a religious sister and a religious nun are that both profess vows of poverty, chastity, and obedience as a path to becoming more like Jesus, who is our model for holiness of life. We also live a life of prayer in community among our sisters, which offers both joys and challenges. Our rough edges are smoothed over as we bump into one another in community along this shared journey of life leading toward heaven.

The Daughters of St. Paul is an international order of Catholic religious sisters founded in Italy in 1915. Our founder, Blessed Father James Alberione, and our cofoundress, Venerable Mother Thecla Merlo, would tell our sisters that we are contemplatives in action. Mother Thecla always encouraged us to have a heart filled with God and to bring God to all we meet with every means possible. She said, "How beautiful and holy it is to communicate Jesus, whom we want to always carry in the center of our heart." Blessed James Alberione gave us a rich spirituality with a daily prayer life consisting of morning and evening prayer, meditation, Mass, an hour of adoration before the Blessed Sacrament, and an additional half hour of personal prayer. If you add all that up, we spend three hours a day in prayer. And we spend even more time living and working in the community.

I believe Fr. Alberione would be fine calling us #Millennial Nuns, but he would be even more excited with our other known name: #MediaNuns—sisters who proclaim Christ using all forms of media. Today's millennials were born in the 1980s. Blessed James Alberione was also born in the eighties—albeit the 1880s! Fr. Alberione received his inspiration to do something great for the people of the new century when he was at prayer. As a young seminarian, he felt Jesus calling him to use the powerful means of the media to communicate the Good News of the Gospel. How prophetic that call turned out to be as the twentieth century exploded with so many inventions of new means of media: press, radio, film, video, DVD, CD, podcasting, social media, digital media, and more. Mother Thecla collaborated with Blessed James in starting the Daughters of St. Paul. Teresa Merlo was born in northern Italy and she grew up in a devout Catholic family. At age twenty-one, she heard about Fr. Alberione and his dream to do something for God and for the people of the new century. She accepted his invitation to join the first group of future Daughters of St. Paul without really knowing exactly what she was saying yes to. She was known for her warm heart, deep faith, and trust in God, who was guiding the beginnings of the Daughters of St. Paul through the vision of Blessed Alberione. They set out on a new worldwide mission of proclaiming the message of Jesus and his promise of salvation through the media.

Over a century later, today I see our #MillennialNun Daughters of St. Paul alive and on fire with that same desire to courageously take up the means of communications media to bring a message of hope to a world searching for answers. On any given day you can find our #MillennialNuns using the newest forms of technology to advance our mission, whether it's on their phones checking on the time of their next meeting; opening our Pauline Books and Media Centers, making sure that the chapel is prepared and the iPad checkout registers are ready to receive our customers; or creating a beautiful image and message to post on Instagram. Not only do they use these means with creativity and Gospel values, they are deeply aware of the media's power to influence individuals and societies. The Daughters of St. Paul reflect deeply on how people interact with the media and are formed by it. We pray for all who use the media, especially media producers, and we pray in reparation for all those times media is abused in order to harm.

As you read the stories of these sisters, you will discover that they gave a generous yes to Jesus as he invited them to become Daughters of St. Paul. You will find that they are human and share the same challenges of all millennials. You will also see beacons of light who pray and have a personal relationship with the God who called them. From this relationship, our #MillennialNuns draw strength and inspiration to share their talents as artists, designers, writers, photographers, bloggers, and social media sharers. The #MillennialNun Daughters of St. Paul are icons of hope to me, and I am proud to have them as my younger sisters in religious life. My wish for them is that they find much happiness and fulfillment as Daughters of St. Paul, and that together we bring lots of hope and joy to the world through the witness of our lives as women consecrated to God.

A further disclaimer: I myself am not a millennial. I joined the Daughters of St. Paul in the 1980s as the #MillennialNuns were just entering into the world, and today I feel a close connection to them as their big sister, friend, and mentor. My hope is that you will find your own faith and spirituality strengthened as you read their stories. Perhaps you know a millennial who may be considering a call to religious life—or is even just looking to learn more—and would welcome a copy of this book. I know that when I was discerning my own path in life, I would have loved a book that gave me an inside glimpse into the life and calling of a religious sister. I remember praying to God to give me an obvious sign that becoming a sister was what I was truly meant to do with my life. (I even suggested that he send an angel down with a direct message!) As my journey to the religious life as a Daughter of St. Paul unfolded, I realized that it was in the recurring thoughts about becoming a religious sister that God was whispering an invitation to me. It was also the initial learning about and observing the sisters in action during visits to the community that drew me to return for another visit. I was attracted to the sisters' joy and simplicity of life as they prayed and worked together. I felt right at home among them, and because I was young enough to be able to enter the convent's St. Paul High School as a junior, I thought to myself, *Why not give it a try? What do I have to lose?*

My parents were very supportive of my decision, and I was fortunate to have this support as I discovered that often a young woman does not. It always surprised my mother when she would tell friends that I had entered the convent and the first question they would ask was, "Is she happy?" I can honestly say that once I entered religious life, I felt a deep inner peace and joy in knowing that I was living the life I was created to live. My life as a religious sister is a life of challenge, beauty, love, joy, and hope in the closer following of Jesus, who is always faithful. In the words of our founder, Blessed James Alberione, "One love: Jesus Christ; one burning desire: to give him to souls."

LEARNING THE LANGUAGE

MEETING GOD *through the* VOWS *of* RELIGIOUS LIFE

SR. AMANDA MARIE DETRY, FSP

I had just unscrewed the gas cap of our Pontiac Montana when the hot August wind lunged after my veil and whipped it across my face. Again. I was in my second month of vowed religious life and still adjusting to many things, including my new relationship with nature. I gently brushed my veil as far away from the gas pump as possible and began to fill our tank.

Minutes later, a car pulled up at the neighboring pump. A middle-age man stepped out, saw me fighting to keep my veil from wrapping around the fuel hose, and walked in my direction. My stomach danced. Veil or no veil, I am an introvert; and now, thanks to the infinite creativity of God, I had become an introvert who stood out in a crowd.

"Hey! I have a question for you," the man asked. He took a few steps closer. "What made you want to do that?"

I knew he wasn't asking about the gas fill-up.

I paused for a moment as a million answers welled up in my mind and in my heart. *Lord, what do I say? Where do I begin?* Suddenly every answer vanished—except one. The right one. The *only* one. I looked him in the eyes and gave a shy smile: "Because I'm in love."

My parents named me "Amanda," which is Latin for "she who must be loved." It is a name that is much easier to carry around with me than it is to live out. In fact, the first time I heard what it means, I resisted the definition. It sounded arrogant to my adolescent ears. I *must* be loved? *Really?*

The verb "love" has a necessity and an urgency about it. God actually commands it: "*You shall love* the Lord your God." When I heard these words as a young Catholic, I wondered if love could really be commanded. I further wondered how I should respond to this command when I didn't feel any special affection toward God. He was a distant, bearded figure who asked us to do things and never seemed to offer any feedback—at least not in the way my parents and teachers did. Even if I could conjure up some feelings of love for Him, when would I feel Him love me back?

Some years ago, an astute five-year-old reminded me that love was never meant to be analyzed or dissected like this. Children don't ponder the "command" of love, how necessary love is, or how best to do it. They simply love. I watched this happen during a mission trip to Texas, as my sisters and I spent an evening at the home of good friends of our community. Their young daughter wanted to show me something in the backyard. I followed her outside, and after taking a hard look at whatever she was pointing at, we both were suddenly distracted by the immense ink-black, diamond-studded Texas sky that stretched over our heads. As we cranked our heads back in wonder, the little girl spontaneously uttered three small words: "I love God!" Then she stooped to the ground and started digging a hole in her mother's flower beds. "I love God, too," I whispered after her, but it sounded pathetic rolling off my lips. She had the spontaneity and the heart; I was stumbling after her, trying to keep up.

Children seem to have a natural capacity to speak to God and raise their hearts to Him. How do we all seem to lose this as we grow up? Or perhaps more importantly, how do we get it back?

My life as a religious sister is about learning this language of God—a language not of words, but of life. God's word to us is not a jumble of letters and sounds, but a person: Jesus Christ. As Daughters of Saint Paul, we live our lives in relationship with this Word. We encounter Jesus speaking to us in Scripture, in the Church, and in our everyday experience of being human, and we continually bring our lives into conformity with His so that we, too, might speak of God. Of course, none of us speak this divine language perfectly. The "accent" of our failures and limitations betrays our lack of fluency. But God is generous and eager to teach. His desire to call forth the image of His Son in each one of us is a bit like Gandalf's approach to Bilbo in *The Hobbit*, when Gandalf knocks on Bilbo's door with a startling invitation: "I am looking for someone to share in an adventure that I am arranging, and it's very difficult to find anyone." God is always knocking at our door. We're just not always home to hear it.

Over the years, I have learned to recognize God's "knocks" as ardent but subtle, filled with respect for my free will and love for my humanity. God has knocked on my pursuit of success and achievement, my relationships with others, and the situations that had me most convinced that He was absent. And with each knock, He has invited me to step beyond the constricted Hobbit hole of human understanding and convenience and learn to speak the language of His love—which is nothing less than the poor, chaste, and obedient life of Christ.

I professed the religious vows of poverty, chastity, and obedience for the first time in June of 2019. In doing so, I said yes to the adventure of following Christ more closely and immersing myself in the language of God's love. Jesus has been my Way, Truth, and Life on every twist and turn of this journey, and every day He offers me another glimpse of what it means to love and to be "in love"— which is to say, to be "in *Him.*"

The Language of Poverty

The books made an unceremonious *thud* as they hit the library table. My backpack was next, followed by a laptop and a thermos full of coffee. These would be my companions for the next several hours. My mind was already churning as I pulled up a chair and began to brainstorm several possible directions for my history paper. Minutes later, my fingers began their rhythmic scramble across my keyboard, punching out the results of my research on the political and gendered leanings of sixteenth-century British periodicals. After an hour of writing, my brain began to drift more pensively over the task at hand; then it stopped entirely.

What was I doing?

It was my junior year of college and my postgraduate dreams were supposedly at their peak. I had spent the prior two years solidifying my decision to double-major in English literature and history. I had a full-tuition scholarship to the University of Wisconsin–Madison, worked part-time for the university honors program advising office, and was presently enjoying life as an exchange student at the University of Warwick in Coventry, England. I was taking a full load of classes, volunteering at a local elementary school, and had recently codirected some scenes of an amateur Shakespeare performance at a British pub. Back home in Wisconsin, I kept equally busy as a writing tutor, a Saint Vincent de Paul Society volunteer, submissions reviewer for the campus humanities journal, and an active member of the Catholic student organization. I went to Mass daily, slept very little, and was keeping my eyes peeled for a career that could integrate my eclectic mix of hobbies and passions, my personality, and my faith. I was struggling to find it.

I had too many interests, too little time, and a rapidly growing fear that my life could not contain everything I wanted to do and to be. Much like the history paper in front of me, I longed to organize the details of my life in a way that communicated something strong, clear, and meaningful. Scholarship committees expected this kind of clearsightedness. Employers wanted to know what I stood for and why they should hire me. I wanted to articulate my purpose, too—but choosing one path meant refusing another, and both actions made me hesitate. I feared that by choosing, I would lose a piece of myself through the cracks between my options, and I didn't know if I would get it back.

After several minutes of mulling over my predicament in the library that afternoon, a new possibility quietly emerged. There was no warning, no context, no obvious trigger for it. It was simply there: *consecrated life.*

I was raised Catholic. My family went to Mass on Sundays, prayed before meals, and participated in our parish religious education program. I loved God as a child, but in my tweens and teens, my relationship with God grew more strained. I still believed in Him and pursued Him; I just wasn't sure how He felt about me. During my first year of university, however, I was deeply impressed by the students I met at our campus Catholic center. They didn't speak about Jesus as a historical person; they spoke about Him as someone they had just had an intimate conversation with. God wasn't some distant, hazy figure to them but a Father who actively provided for His children, and whose providence they could see, feel, and touch. They were radiant, and I envied them. If God loved them enough to make them so keenly aware of His presence, why wasn't He doing the same for me? I wondered what I was doing wrong—or what might be wrong with me.

My doubts pushed me to approach faith as something "I" needed to do better. I began to schedule more time for prayer, including daily Mass. I gave God room in my academic planner and hoped He would speak to me in the time I offered Him. Occasionally I thought I heard Him; most of the time I wasn't sure. Prayer felt like a lot of guesswork. I just hoped God would give me points for effort. In the meantime, I scrambled to fill my planner with the rest of the things I needed to accomplish: school, work, extracurriculars, social life, exercise, grocery shopping, and sleep. Sometimes I felt as if I were holding all the components of my life in a flimsy paper bag that was about to burst at the seams. I was terrified of what would happen if the bag split.

So when the idea of consecrated life suddenly flashed through my mind in the Warwick College library, I was taken aback. This was not an invitation to schedule or accomplish something; it was an invitation to *be someone*. To be "consecrated" was to belong to God, to be set apart for Him and at His service. Could I *do* that? Like, officially? My pragmatic mind wrestled with the idea, unconvinced yet irresistibly compelled by it. It lured my mind away from academic prose and threw it into the realm of poetry. The thought of consecration did not connote a task or a goal; it whispered a promise.

I looked around the library. My peers were squinting into their books and computer screens, eager to digest a few more facts and formulas for their year-end exams. I should have been joining them, but instead I googled "consecrated life." I found a blog written by a young woman who had just professed religious vows. And I read.

She was about my age: twenty-five years old to my twenty-one. She wrote about belonging to God and loving Him completely, with all her strength and being. She spoke of Christ as the unifying purpose and center of her life. Most powerfully of all, she seemed to be living what she wrote about. God's love was not just an idea to her, but a tangible reality that inspired a radical response. Her reflection was short, but her words lit a fire in my heart.

I can still taste the freedom that surged forth from deep within my chest that day, relieving me of the load I was carrying. God knew the endless string of hopes, dreams, gifts, and limitations I held inside of me. He had put them there. He loved each one of them. More importantly, He loved me. I understood that the more I tried to obsessively plan and arrange (and rearrange) my life's options, the more anxious I would grow and the further I would be from Him. Jesus was not just one part of my life. He *was* my life— its origin and its destination—and I would never fully know myself or my calling except through Him.

I left the library that day with no clear insights into my future. I didn't even have a finished history paper. All I had was a new and unwavering assurance that God saw me, knew me, loved me, and had something in mind for me—possibly religious life. In the months that followed, I also began to realize that if I wanted to make room for a Love as great as this, I would need to let go of some things.

A short time later, one of my professors in Wisconsin emailed to ask if I had ever considered applying for a Rhodes Scholarship. She thought I had potential and was willing to offer me her mentorship, if I was interested. I swallowed—hard. This should have been the opportunity I was waiting for, but the level of competition I knew it would require threatened to throw me right back to where I was before: as an ambitious college junior making up life as I went, rather than a young woman beginning to discover and live more authentically the life God had already given me. I declined.

Not long after, a professor at Warwick called me into her office. "I enjoy your work," she began as I took a seat across from her. "You understand what we do here. If you wanted to come back for graduate school, I would love to work with you." I was moved by her offer. I also knew that if I said yes, it would be my ego speaking and not my true self. Slowly but surely, I was learning to detect the difference. There was a part of me who longed to define myself through advancement and achievement, but the real "me," awakened by the Word of God, discerned that this was unnecessary. God knew me through and through. If I wanted to know myself and the meaning of my life, I could not hope to find them in a career or an award. I needed to pursue God and reject whatever might distract me from this pursuit. I needed to learn how to say no, so that I could say yes to the God who held my past, present, and future in His embrace.

This yes to God is the language and entire lexicon of poverty. When we speak of poverty, we often think about the no's, but the no means absolutely nothing if it does not enable us to say yes to God from the depths of our being, with all that we are.

The power of this yes—and the many no's it requires—is impossible to exaggerate in a world that urges us to keep all our options open, refrain from commitment, change our minds frequently, "go with the flow," and scroll indeterminately through social media to relieve our FOMO. This is the yes of the major life commitments of marriage, consecrated life, and priestly ordination, as well as the small, day-to-day yesses we make for love of Christ.

Saint Paul, the patron of our Congregation, explains this dynamic best in his letter to the Philippians: "Have among yourselves the same mind that is in Christ Jesus, who, though He was in the form of God, did not regard equality with God something to be grasped; rather, He emptied Himself . . ." (Philippians 2:6–7). I prayed with this passage one afternoon while I was discerning whether to enter the Daughters of St. Paul. As I did, I found myself savoring the humility of Christ and the challenge He offers us. Jesus does not "grasp" and preach His identity as God, even though it rightly belongs to Him. Far from it. He is utterly unrecognizable on the Cross, not only as God but—thanks to the brutality of Roman beatings—as a human being as well. Why would the Son of God allow Himself to be subjected to such gross misrepresentation and misunderstanding? Because Jesus entrusted His identity, reputation, and entire being to His Father, and not to the world.

His yes to God was so complete, He allowed God to raise Him up to His rightful place as Son and Savior in His own time.

This is poverty.

In the consecrated life, our identity is not composed of the things we do, the roles we have been given, the opinions others have of us, or even the attitudes we have about ourselves. We may be tempted to cling to one or all of these things in an effort to tell the world (or ourselves) who we are, but this possessive attitude distracts our gaze from where it ought to be—on God the Father. Like Jesus, we must reserve our yes for God and the daily invitations He offers us to grow in love, patience, trust, humility, and hope. We must also have the courage to offer a full-throated no to every other offer. We cannot "have it all" in this world (sorry, Jason Mraz), nor should we want to, because if we strive for everything, we will end up with nothing. On the other hand, if we view every situation as an opportunity to choose what will best help us love and imitate Christ, we *will* choose All—and this choice will be all the more powerful because of every no we utter in the process.

The Language of Chastity

My first visit to a convent was in the quaint village of Brownshill, England. I was not discerning a religious vocation at the time; I just wanted a weekend to pray, rest, and see another part of England. I carpooled with some friends to get there, and as our van rolled over the gentle, winding slopes of the British countryside, I marveled at the world we were entering. Away from the bustle of the university campus, this hilltop Bernardine Cistercian monastery felt like something out of a Wordsworth poem. I was enchanted.

One morning that weekend, after celebrating Mass together, my friends, some of the sisters, and I knelt in the convent chapel for a few extra minutes of silent prayer. One by one, everyone stood up and left. Except me.

As I knelt in front of the tabernacle where the Blessed Sacrament, the Real Presence of Christ, was reserved, I was suddenly acutely aware of the Lord's presence. Jesus was physically *here* in front of me. And He wasn't just sitting here; He was dynamic and alive. I was drawn to Him, forcefully yet gently, and in the ineffable mystery of that moment, I understood that I was feeling some of the weight of God's endless love. It pressed upon me, and I didn't resist. I could not fight it, even if I wanted to. I was in a state of contradiction, both at peace and not at peace, overwhelmed by the passion that surrounded me, yet calm enough to remain where I was. I was loved. Immensely loved. *Fearfully* loved. And through the terrifying beauty of such love, a word of Scripture suddenly emerged and pressed itself against the ear of my heart: "Love others as I have loved you."

This was the first time I grasped the sheer *impossibility* of God's command. How could I love as perfectly as God loved?

I don't know how long I was in the chapel, though I do remember leaving in somewhat of a daze. As I pushed open the chapel doors, I saw a sister standing in the hall outside, talking to one of my friends. I looked at both of them with a mix of reverence, wonder, and fear. God loved them immensely. And me? What could I do? Say? Everything felt so insufficient, and I stood there dumbly, a little frozen by the hopelessness of it all.

As my friend walked away, the sister looked over at me and smiled. "You really love the Lord, don't you?" My face turned as red as my ginger hair. *Had she seen me in the chapel?* I wondered. *What had she seen?*

I returned her gaze sheepishly and let out a lame, but honest response: "I ... try to."

Sister smiled wider. "Don't try so hard."

I am a chronic perfectionist—which is precisely why I trembled my way out of the Brownshill chapel that morning. God had given me an impossible command, and the certainty of failure stopped me in my tracks. That sister's words, however—"Don't try so hard"— gently redirected my gaze from my obvious human weakness to the abundant generosity of God. God was not asking me to compete with His love; He was inviting me to accept and surrender to it. He wasn't calling me to love others *for* Him, but *with* Him.

Years later, as I began to pray more intentionally about my vocation, my introspective anxiety returned with a vengeance. Despite my attraction to the religious life and to the Daughters of St. Paul, I just wasn't convinced that such a radical choice was ... well, *necessary*. How did I know, without a doubt, that God really wanted this from me? Wasn't it arrogant to think that God would ask *me* to belong to Him and communicate His love to the world? As the months went by, I began to pray for an unmistakable sign that I was called to be a Daughter of St. Paul. Prudence (not love) told me that I could not say yes until I had absolute clarity.

Such "clarity" came almost one year later through an un-expected phone call: a friend from my parish young adult group wanted to ask me out. This was not an earth-shattering question, but to my ears, it sounded like an ultimatum. For some reason, I had assumed God would clear up my confusion about the future before any dating possibilities appeared on my horizon. And now? Now I had to concretely choose something without the clarity and assurance I had prayed for. I didn't like it.

I was on my way home to visit family in Michigan when the call came through. Oddly grateful for my lack of availability, I postponed my friend's invitation and boarded my flight with even more on my mind than I had anticipated. When I reached Detroit, I spent my layover pacing the airport from Terminal A to Terminal C, and back again, wondering what to say when I called him back.

I wanted to say yes. Dating felt safer, more comfortable, and frankly more normal than religious life. I was excited about the possibility of falling in love and didn't want to miss this chance. And yet . . . somehow, the door to religious life still felt open. As I paced and prayed with my roller luggage, I began to realize that God wasn't going to clear things up for me. He was offering me a choice—and He wanted *me* to choose.

Until that moment, I had been willing to enter the Daughters of St. Paul as long as I knew that this was what God wanted. If it wasn't necessary, I wasn't going to do it. What I hadn't considered was that God might invite me to be part of the decision. God was opening two doors for me, religious life and marriage, and was patiently waiting for me to step through one of them. Moved by God's gentleness, I realized deep down that I wanted to say yes to Him through the vows of religious life, and that I longed for His yes in return. Perhaps the vows *were* unnecessary and over-the-top—but then again, so was God's love for me.

I applied to the Daughters of St. Paul a few weeks later. As I did, my obsession with discovering the will of God faded into a deeper understanding that God rarely reveals His will to us in full color and graphic detail. He leads us step-by-step and invites us to follow. He calls and leaves us free to respond. The choice is always ours, and so is the joy of making a choice not for the sake of security or clarity, but for love of God.

The Language of Obedience

Blessed James Alberione, the founder of our Congregation, once wrote that "obedience is the greatest freedom." A paradox? Perhaps. But at age nineteen, I learned that it could also be true.

Midway through my first semester of college, I was diagnosed with anorexia. The disease had been slowly and insidiously attack‑ing my mind and my body for nearly a year, but I had not recognized it—at least not directly. Most sufferers don't.

I was obliquely aware that *something* was happening, of course. In the year leading up to my diagnosis, I had gradually stopped eat‑ing and my mental health was deteriorating. The smallest inconve‑nience was powerful enough to send me spiraling into a depression or kindle a rage so intense I barely managed to hide it away. As friends and family questioned my apparent weight loss and trou‑bled mood, I assured them I was fine, while secretly holding to the conviction that I needed to be better, and thinner, than I was.

Eventually I ended up in the university medical center and was gently coerced into seeing three different specialists in between my freshman classes. They gave me one goal: to try to gain back one pound per week. Three weeks later, I had lost another pound. As my doctor logged the disappointing weigh‑in on his clipboard, he turned to me with a suggestion that took my breath away. "You might want to take the next semester off of school to work on your health." I was stunned. To quit school was to admit I had a problem, and I still didn't fully believe that something was wrong.

"Absolutely not," I fired back. "I can do this. It's just . . ." I trailed off, lost in the effort to verbalize my frustration. "I thought I was supposed to listen to my body, and my body is never hungry. So why eat? If I'm really supposed to eat more, why isn't my body tell‑ing me that?" Each question dripped with anger, fear, and my recur‑ring doubt that anything was even wrong in the first place. They were not really questions about eating, but questions about what to believe.

"Your body isn't hungry because you're not eating," the doctor replied. I stared blankly at him, turning the paradox over in my mind with a mix of curiosity and disgust. He went on. "You have to teach your brain how to be hungry again. You've starved it for so long that it's no longer responding the way it's supposed to respond. You can't wait to be hungry before you start eating; you have to eat first. Then you will feel hungry."

This conversation was the turning point in my recovery from anorexia—and in many ways, it has become a foundational metaphor for my relationship with God as well. Beneath the doctor's words was something more than an invitation to eat. It was a call to obey a truth that I didn't fully believe yet, with the promise that I *would* believe—and heal—if I dared to live it anyway. It was my own personal experience of Jesus calling me out of the boat to walk on water toward Him. The waves threatened to overwhelm me, and yet the voice of our Lord—"Come"—was unmistakable and had the power to help me walk.

When I left the medical office, I bought a Venti Starbucks chocolate banana smoothie and muscled it down my throat in obedience. I was terrified, but deep down, I knew that obedience to my doctor's orders was my salvation, even as my twisted emotions and disordered reasoning told me otherwise.

A few months later, I left campus for a weekend to visit a friend in another city. She had taken up ballroom dancing and invited me to go to salsa practice with her. Open to the adventure, I borrowed her dress pants and joined her in the middle of the dance floor, mimicking the instructor's footing and watching my movements in the mirror to check my accuracy. Suddenly I stopped. I locked eyes with myself in the mirror for the first time in a long time, and I finally saw what everyone else had been seeing: how thin, and how sick, I really was. It was the first time I really believed the truth of my illness, and I instinctively knew this gift of sight was the fruit of the past several months of slow, tedious acts of obedience to my doctor and faith in the promise of a healthier life. I had been a prisoner of my illness and disordered thinking, but obedience to the truth was setting me free.

In the spiritual life, the call to obedience is ultimately a call to listen—deeply, honestly, and with humility—in order to know and live in the Truth. As Christians, we believe in a God who continually speaks to us through Scripture, the life and teachings of the Church, and the events of daily life. If we want to know God *as He is* (and ourselves as *we* really are, since we are made in His image), we must be attentive to the ways God reveals Himself to us and follow the plan of life that He proposes. This often means trusting God and His commandments even when they don't immediately make sense to us. After all, God transcends our human ways of knowing. His Word is not designed to fit comfortably within our current lifestyle, emotional state, and flawed human reasoning. Quite the opposite. God speaks to release us from our limitations, so that by trusting and living His Word, we might have a share in His life, sentiments, and knowledge. God always calls us to Himself, and that means traveling beyond *ourselves*. The more we follow God's call across the tight boundaries we draw around our life, the more we discover that His Word is not just a simple commandment or teaching. The Word is Jesus Himself, who lives in us through our obedience. As our lives increasingly mirror the life of Jesus, we learn to see Him as He is and ourselves as we really are. And this truth sets us free.

When I entered the Daughters of St. Paul in my mid-twenties, I arrived with tight personal boundaries and stereotypical expectations. I was eager to experience God through the life, prayer, and mission of my new community and didn't think I would have to look too hard to find Him. As I got to know the three women I had entered with, however, I was taken aback by how *different* we were—and how easy it was for us to get on each other's nerves. All four of us had entered the community with different sets of life experiences, family cultures, and expectations about religious life that we were individually trying to "obey." They didn't always dovetail, and misunderstandings and tensions seemed to abound.

After several months of this, I was suddenly knocked down by a wave of homesickness. I missed *my* people and *my* friends, whom I naturally understood and got along with. What was the Lord asking of me here? I had followed Him into the convent, and now He seemed to have left me at the doorstep. After one particularly difficult day, I walked into our chapel for my daily hour of Adoration and started fuming. It wasn't much of a prayer, more of a complaint-ridden monologue. I didn't expect Jesus to respond, and part of me wondered if He was even listening. I was stunned into silence, therefore, when the Lord interrupted my prayer with a question of His own: "What do you need that I have not provided for you? Tell me what you need, and I will give it."

Rarely have I heard Jesus speak to me so clearly in prayer as He did that day. I did not hear Him with my ears, but His question cut through my tangled, emotion-laden thoughts with unmistakable precision. I paused and gingerly considered Jesus' question. What struck me the most was the *way* He asked it. Jesus' words weren't huffy, as I might have said them. ("Seriously, Amanda? What do you *still* need that I haven't given you already?") Rather, He asked with longing and a desire to fulfill: *Tell me what you need.* I revisited my grumbling to figure out what, exactly, I needed from Him. In the end, I found nothing. I had everything I needed; just not everything I *wanted.* And what I especially wanted was a group of women I could get along with a little more easily.

Jesus then offered me two more words: "Trust me." Through them, I understood that Jesus was revealing Himself to me through these women. He was loving me in ways I wasn't used to being loved, through women whose hearts were different from my own—and yet very much the same. It was not enough for me to experience love in the way I was "used to" experiencing it. Jesus wanted my heart to resemble His own, and to do this, He needed to stretch it. Every moment of every day was a new opportunity to obey His invitation to give and receive love in new ways, beyond the tight boundaries of my own culture, upbringing, and understanding. I could dismiss the things I didn't understand as obstacles to following God, or I could believe God was present in the very people and moments that perplexed me the most, and listen for His invitation to love Him *there* and receive His love in new and unexpected ways.

We often think of the will of God as something that is "out there" for us to find. But God does not hide His will from us. It is always here, taking concrete form in the situations, people, history, and circumstances that surround us. This is the context in which God urges us to "step out of the boat" of our current understanding, trust in the truth of His Word, and follow Him. When we do so, He lifts the veil on His promise to be with us always and allows us to glimpse where and how He is at work in our lives. And in the same breath, He beckons us to follow Him higher, further, and deeper still.

The Language of Love

The Daughters of St. Paul have been singing and recording albums for years, as part of our mission to proclaim Christ through media. A couple years ago, my superiors asked if I would join the choir. The request took me by surprise. I had limited talent and no experience to speak of, unless you count car karaoke. I was willing, but skeptical.

Thankfully, one of my sisters saw my plight and offered to give me some singing lessons and breathing tips. As we met in her office one afternoon, she helped me with my posture, led me through vocal warm-ups, and taught me how to project my voice from the right part of my face. I exhaled several notes at a medium volume while carefully eyeing her office window and the hallway outside.

"Sing out!" she gently encouraged.

"I'm really not a good singer," I confessed, turning away from the window and meeting her gaze. "I don't know why they asked me to do this."

She nodded in understanding. "I felt the same way when they first asked me to join the choir. I'm not confident in my voice either. But if the sisters chose you, they obviously see something you don't see."

There it was again: the call to trust, to obey, to step out of the boat and meet Jesus in a place I had never intended to go.

My sister continued, as if she had read my thoughts. "I've come to realize that singing is ultimately an act of love. We can't hear our voice the way others hear it; it resonates differently in our ears than it does for them. We sing, not because we want to know what we sound like or how good we are, but because we offer the gift of our voice to the Lord and trust that He will use it as He desires. This is our gift to Him and to His People—and if God is going to use it, we have to let go of what we think about ourselves."

It is easy to harbor anxiety about how others see and respond to us. It is easy to make comparisons and judgments; to internalize the praise and the doubts that others voice about us; and to calculate whether the return we get is worth the effort we put into trying to communicate something to the world. It is much harder to "sing out" in love without looking for something in return. Nevertheless, this is precisely the kind of singing Christ models for us through His life of poverty, chastity, and obedience. The life of Christ is a song of selfless love and freedom, and it is taken up by those who have nothing to lose because they are secure in the knowledge that they are children of God. If we want to learn this song and hear its melody in the background of our lives, we have to practice singing it: not by our own efforts, but in communion with the Holy Spirit who has promised to teach us His language of love and attune our hearts to its everlasting cadence.

Our world needs more singers. It needs men and women who are not afraid to give God more than what they think others will understand, so that others may see in them a reflection of the God beyond all understanding. The world needs the gift of our voices and our lives, so that it might find in us—as my sisters and I have found in Christ—a language of life through which it, too, can lift the fullness of its heart to God.

NOTES ON EMBRACING THE MOMENT

Sr. Tracey Dugas, FSP

But I'm Not a Writer

In my life as a religious sister, it is not unusual for complete strangers to walk up to me, tell me deeply personal things, and then ask me to pray for them. Many times, they are perfectly content with a promise of prayer and we go our separate ways. Other times they haltingly ask, "Can you pray now?" So right there in the cereal aisle of the grocery store, we pray.

What *is* unusual is to have a random stranger make a particular effort to pray for me . . . and tell me things that only God can know.

One day at our convent in New Orleans, I happened to be cooking lunch when another sister, one who is not easily swayed by flashy religiosity, came to the kitchen with the most earnest look on her face and said, "Sister. I think you should go downstairs. We have a visitor and he is asking to pray with you."

She explained that Jim was a gentleman who was doing Christian ministry in the area with his team and had stopped at our Pauline Books and Media Center for a short visit. He had become active in ministry after a near-death experience brought with it an added spiritual gift: Jim had been given a gift of prophesy. Despite the commonly held idea that prophesy means to tell the future, the spiritual gift of prophesy, in the Catholic sense, is to see the world as God sees the world. Jim had a gift for speaking a special word of revelation from God to the person for whom he prayed. He was offering to pray with me.

Sister continued, "I think you should let Jim pray with you."

I was skeptical. "Really? Why?"

She closed her eyes and said, "Because he just prayed with me and told me something that only God could know. I really think his gift is from God."

I had nothing to lose. I turned off all the burners on the stove and went downstairs. Jim was standing there, waiting for me. He asked me to hold out my hands and join him in praying to receive what the Lord wanted to give me. He then lightly touched my hands and said, "The Lord is showing me that you are a beautiful writer."

That's it? I thought. *Of all the things God could've used this guy to tell me, he chose this?*

I am no writer.

As a member of the Daughters of Saint Paul, I belong to a

religious congregation with a mission of spreading faith through communication and media. We have many sisters who write, but I'm not one of them. Thankfully for me, this mission allows for a multitude of ways of sharing the Gospel. Some sisters are authors, some sing, some create art, and some are present through social media. I've discovered that one of my gifts is the spoken word. Put me in front of people, whether it's one or one hundred, in a relaxed or formal setting, and I will have something to say, especially if it's about the love of God. But if you want me to write about it, to put it down on paper, I get stuck. I can't even start. I know that about myself.

So I thanked Jim, and I left it at that.

Jim's words came back to me as I received the invitation to contribute a chapter to this book. My hope was that maybe this time writing wouldn't be so difficult. All I had to do was simply share my story. I pictured myself getting a brilliant idea, becoming totally inspired, and then writing and writing until I was done. There would be an inspiration and a flow. Yep, just get me going, and before you know it, I will have written the best chapter ever.

Inspiration did not come. What came instead was one of the most traumatic years of the last century: a pandemic, riots and looting of our convent in downtown Chicago, huge upheaval in both my ministry and my life. To put it frankly: it's been one of the weirdest years I've ever experienced.

After months and months of trying and failing to write, and exhausted by the turmoil of 2020, I needed some time away from the city to get my head and heart straight. I needed to find a safe way to be alone, gather my thoughts, and work on this project. I found out that we sisters have a friend of the community who built a cabin on her property and the sisters stayed with her on one of their missionary trips. After a short phone call, I was graciously given a full week to rest at a chicken farm in the middle of Illinois.

Right Where You Are

On my first day there, grateful for the respite, I curl up on the sofa and notice a book by Ann Voskamp that I've been wanting to read: *One Thousand Gifts*. The subtitle catches me: *A Dare to Live Fully Right Where You Are*. I nearly throw the book across the room.

Right where you are. I am here with the chickens to get *away* from "right where you are." I wanted to scream: *What if right where you are is exactly NOT where I want to be, Ann? What if right where you are is hard and you feel like a failure and all you can do is stare at the chickens?* (Who, by the way, happen to be amazingly interesting creatures to watch. Plus, the fresh eggs are the bomb.) How could Ms. Voskamp dare me to live *this* fully?

Like it or not, this was my now and I had to face it. God allowed me to find that book so that he could point me back to a deep inner value that I hold very dear: embrace reality. I've always been convinced of the fact that God is most present to me in reality, in the very moment in which I am living. Living in the moment, being present to reality, has been a deep and foundational truth in my life and in my relationship with God. If I'm present to whoever and whatever is right in front of me, my feet are planted on the ground and I find my center. It is a lesson that has brought me home to myself, over and over again. It has paved the way to peace in very painful situations, and it has connected me to other people, especially in their "otherness." Above all, receiving what's right in front of me has connected me to God.

Just when I think I've learned something for good, life comes with a new gut check. Right now, I need to embrace reality. I need to face 2020, be present to the present, live fully the moment I'm living in. I feel like I am being asked to give what I don't feel I have. Somehow, I have to deal with this hard thing that's right in front of me when all I really want to do is run away from it. The question is: *Am I willing to learn how to receive what's being given right here, right now?*

In this past year especially, it has become increasingly easy to reject what we don't like and only accept those persons or realities that please us or agree with us. We live in a cancel culture. If you don't like something, you cancel it. If you see enough posts on social media that argue with your own take on things, you unfollow that account. If the media portrays a version of reality that argues with what you know, you protest it, disassociate from it, or rebuke it. There are myriads of ways to turn our backs to that which we don't like.

But ultimately, the "otherness" remains. They are still them and you are still you.

Things might fall just outside our expectations or they might spiral completely out my control. So what to do? Do you cancel, cut off, and run away from things you don't like? Or do you press in, receive reality for what it is, and find a way to live with it? If you do, then some real lessons can be learned about receiving reality. Especially when it's terrifying.

Jim's prophetic words, "You are a beautiful writer," have not made my reality any easier. But if they are really from God, I have to remember that there is a power in the Word of God over reality. God speaks things into creation. In the beginning of time, God sent his Spirit over the unformed chaos and spoke his creative Word over it. God's Word brought forth what did not yet exist. When God said, "Let there be light," there was light. Like it or not, God is calling me to be a writer for you, dear reader. What follows is not a cohesive essay or a straight narrative. I offer instead vignettes of my life, vignettes in which I've had to learn how to embrace what I'm being given and dare to live fully right where I am.

So, it appears to me that whatever the answer is lies somewhere in writing it down. So, okay, God. I'll be your writer. But I'm leaving the "beautiful" to you.

Beautiful, Harsh Reality

Once I was invited to share some spiritual reflections to a group of recovering drug addicts and their family members. It was my first time attending a meeting similar to Alcoholics Anonymous. Normally, whenever I was invited to speak to a group, I would do some prep work by noting what I wanted to say, paying attention to what was shared with me, and reminding myself to speak from my heart. In the weeks prior to this event, I had spoken to other small groups about grace and mercy, so I decided to pull out those notes and speak from that. Simple enough.

The meeting began with the group of about fifteen adults introducing themselves and sharing how they were doing. The group was varied; there were married couples, young adult women, parents, grandparents . . . some looked pained, some were fidgety, some expectant. To start, I was invited to share a few words. So I opened my Scriptures to Ephesians 2 and read aloud a passage that spoke about how Jesus is the peace we are all looking for. I then talked about grace and how we need Jesus to provide what we can't provide for ourselves. How we have needs that only God can fill.

Afterward, a few people spoke about what struck them in what I had to say. Then a young man, Jason, walked in, sat next to a man I'll call George, whom I'd met at a prior speaking engagement. The young guy began to weep. George asked him what was going on and he said that he was sorry he was late. He was feeling pretty bad that day and hadn't really wanted to come to the gathering but decided to do so because he knew he was supposed to. He went on to say that he was very tempted to drink, adding, "I really want to kill myself. I'm not a good person. I'm a very bad person."

George put his right arm around him, thanked him, then

turned to me and said, "You see this, Sister? Sometimes we come to these meetings all prepared with our little talk, trying to say something we think others want to hear from us. And sometimes we come like Jason here. Broken and scared. All he has to give is who he is. He's not fixed up. He's just who he is. And he's here, like the rest of us are here. He's here to listen and maybe learn something."

The whole time that he spoke, George never took his eyes off me. I felt horrible, like my worst nightmare was happening; like every fear I'd ever felt was being realized. There are many occasions as a religious person where you feel how inadequate you are to the task of leading people to God, when you feel like a fraud. For me, this was definitely one of them.

My brother told me a hard truth once, a truth that felt especially relevant in this moment: "Just 'cause you wear a 'do-rag' [referring to my veil] and people call you Sister doesn't make you any better than the rest of us." He was right. And George could see that, too. It felt like George could see straight through me. I wanted to disappear, run, be anywhere but there.

But something else was happening.

Deeper down than all that shame and shock, I was very calm, which surprised me. I felt myself get very quiet and a strange peace came over me. Even though I was sure that I was going to melt into the floor from being called out like that, I also weirdly felt blessed. I knew that I really did need to listen, to listen to that moment. To be present to this terrifying present because I really did want to learn.

I went home that night and asked the Lord to help me receive what I was being given, as terrifying as it was. "I want you to keep listening to him. Call him," I felt the Lord say.

Ew, really?

I called George a few days later and thanked him for what he had told me. At first, he said he didn't really recall his remarks. But seeming to remember, he said, "Sister, I was having a bad night and I think I took it out on you. I'm so sorry."

But then he added, "When I first started going to these meet-ings, all I would share were lies. It took me a long, long time to even want to be different. Sister, don't fall into telling people what you think they want to hear. Just show them who you are and what you're really living. People like me need to know that it's okay to be messed up sometimes. Let us know that we can come together and be who we really are and that we won't die from it. Because God knows that all we want to do and all our bodies want us to do, is to numb the pain. We have learned how to run away through alcohol, drugs, addictions, but the problems are still there when we sober up. And many times, we've made them worse by hiding ourselves from them.

"For us, living in the truth is about life and death. If we don't learn how to *find a home in the truth*, then we die. Sometimes truth means that you have nothing to say. Sometimes it means that you're here to listen and to learn. If that's what you are, then be that."

Good Lord, George.

"Sister, I went to two of your other talks. And I heard you speak about basically the same thing you told us. I'm sorry I was so harsh. But I needed to tell you that I didn't want your leftovers. I needed you to give me what you are actually living with God. If you're not living something with God, then you have nothing to say."

Lost for words, I thanked him, and we hung up. It was one of the most difficult, terrifying, and enlightening gifts anyone has ever given me.

Receiving What's Given

Every person is built to give and to receive. Both of these dynamics greatly factor into our daily lives and it's easy to move right past them without much reflection on what these dynamics have to teach us.

Mary, the Mother of Jesus, is a great model of the concept of receptivity. She opened herself to receiving God in such a radical way that God took flesh within her. She made room for a new life to develop within her, which in turn opened her up to make room for others around her.

One way that Catholics understand Mary is to call her the New Eve. The first Eve had the chance to receive who she was and what she was called to do by trusting God. However, when the serpent threw doubt on God's goodness and intentions, Eve refused to receive the word of her Creator. Instead, she doubted what she knew of God and his plan for her. Eve failed to trust in God's timing, God's will, God's way of giving her something good. In short, she was unreceptive.

Mary's example as the New Eve teaches that receptivity allows us to receive the truth from God. She is able to see herself as God sees her and give of herself as a gift. When we receive the presence of God as it is revealed to us in our reality, we are able to receive him within us, receive others, and receive the present moment in a redemptive way.

Receptivity is an essential quality of the spiritual life. While it can easily appear to be passive and a bit weak under cursory observation, true receptivity is the active capacity to accept and welcome that which is being offered you. It also entails harnessing the freedom to let it go when the time comes to do so. Receptivity is the opposite of grasping, manipulating, or controlling. Receiving what's being given means living in truth. It means being authentic and being at home in who you really are.

Through prayer and study, I've deepened my understanding of the place of receptivity in my life, both physically and spiritually. Learning how to receive has made me more attentive to life's mysteries, so that I can actively accept what's being offered, even if it's difficult to take in the moment.

Beauty that Lasts

Growing up, especially as a teenager, I believed that being happy and successful had nothing to do with being authentic and receiving my truth. I believed I had to improve upon the truth. I had to conform myself to the images of beauty, success, and achievement I saw in society, especially as they came to me in magazines and movies. I was convinced that if I looked a certain way and did all the things that made you popular, I would connect with the right people and then I would finally be happy.

The only problem was that it took so much work to try to meet that ideal. I had acne, which required loads of time layering concealer, which in turn made me feel insecure. I hung out with the popular kids

but quickly began to question my choices when we ended up doing idiotic things "for fun." I'd go to the mall to buy the latest outfit, only to frustratingly find that what was "in" this week was "out" next week. It was exhausting and demoralizing. Was there anyone or anything that could provide me the joy I wanted in a way that really lasted?

I was raised Catholic, but my family's faith mainly consisted of going to Mass on Sundays and giving something up for Lent. I went to public school, but after seeing that the parish youth group included fun trips, I joined. One day, I was asked by a friend to go to something I'd never experienced. "Hey, Tracey, you want to come with us to a youth retreat tonight?"

I didn't even know what a retreat was. I politely declined because I didn't know who else was going. What if only the losers went? God forbid I'd mix myself up with any of them.

But as so often happens with teenagers, gossip spread and I found out that the guy I had a crush on would be there. If he'd be there, then I'd have a place to stare.

"Okay, I guess I'll come."

When I arrived at the parish center the day of the retreat, I was dressed to impress. I scanned the room to find my crush. After spotting him, I made sure to sit behind him so that I could keep my eye on him throughout the night. I was very focused on making a good impression. *How's my hair? Do I still have lipstick on? Do I look like I'm one of the cool people?*

In the midst of my jumbled thoughts, twelve college-age young people ran out from behind our seated group and introduced themselves by acting out some of the funniest, most self-deprecating skits I had ever seen. I later found out that they were traveling youth missionaries, crisscrossing the country to offer spiritual retreats to teens. While being surprisingly entertained, I noticed something, especially about the girls on the team. They didn't seem to care in the least about what they looked like. They centered their attention on something else entirely. They were focused on us, the retreatants.

At first, I felt sorry for them. I thought, it must really be awful to not look your best every day. But watching them carefully, I began to realize that they were genuinely happy to be right where they were. With us. They had found lasting happiness by having God in their lives and they were willing to make sacrifices to be able to share his love with teenage strangers like us.

They had freely given up a year of their lives to be missionaries. They traded sleeping in normal beds for spending the night in sleeping bags in the homes of host families. They gave up a decent wardrobe and wore the same set of simple clothes every day. They gave up choosing when and where they wanted to eat, to consume the food that was provided for them (most of the time it was lasagna). They sacrificed all of these good things so that strangers like me could hear about how life-changing it was to put God at the center of your life.

As I watched them, it hit me that I wanted God to be the center of my life, too. I wanted to be about something so real and true that I could be free to be who I really was, no matter who I was with. I was so exhausted trying to be what I thought other people wanted me to be. These youth missionaries were free to receive what was right in front of them. Their relationship with God had set them free to be who they were, wherever they were, whomever they were with. I wanted that. Badly.

Getting Personal

Later that night, the youth team told us that they wanted to pray with each of us individually. I'd never prayed outside of church or with anyone other than my mom before that point. To me, prayer was just reciting the phrases I had memorized as a child. I'd never had such a personal offer and I was nervous. I walked into the dark room and could see silhouettes of the team members with retreatants sitting next to them. I sat next to a girl with red, curly hair named Ann. She whispered to me that she wanted to pray with me to God for whatever I wanted her to pray for.

I had no idea what to tell her.

"Is there anything you're struggling with? Anything you need?"

There's something overwhelming and inexplicable about having a stranger want to speak to God on your behalf. I couldn't believe she was going to do that for me. It completely caught me off guard. I felt I had so many things in my heart that I couldn't pick just one to tell her about.

"I don't want to feel so bad about myself all the time. Sometimes I really hate myself. That's about it."

Ann placed her hand on my shoulder and whispered her prayer

for me. I took a deep breath in, trying to absorb what I was being given. Much to my embarrassment, a huge sob rose up from somewhere deep inside of me. All the weird, intense feelings I'd bottled up as a fifteen-year-old came pouring out. Ann kept quietly praying, and I kept crying. Then I noticed that from the place on my shoulder where she'd placed her hand, a feeling of warmth began to spread through me. Even more deeply, I felt the personal love and acceptance God had for me. I'd never felt something so personal and so beautiful in my life. In the moment, I felt peace, so much peace.

Encountering God for myself in this moment connected me to a desire that was deeper than being the most popular, the most stylish, or the most successful person. What I wanted even more than all of that was simply to be me. I wanted to be happy on the inside. I wanted to feel at home in myself, and for the first time, it really seemed possible.

During that retreat, I was made to understand that whoever has God has peace. I wanted to have that peace. God was showing me that his love for me made me acceptable and I didn't have to strive to achieve it. I just had to live the blessing I had already been given. I just had to receive the person I actually was.

By the end of that retreat, I experienced a wholly different kind of love. I was shown a love that gave me value simply for existing. I truly felt that these missionaries wanted my good for my own sake, independent of anything I could earn or accomplish. They could extend this love because they were willing to love the person right in front of them . . . even if they were strangers. I felt drawn to become the kind of person who could love like that.

put love into everything

Ti Voglio Bene

Years after that retreat, I lived in Italy for almost a year before I professed perpetual vows, and while I was there, I had to learn Italian. One of my favorite things to hear an Italian say was "I love you." Italians actually have a few ways to convey this sentiment. If they mean it in a romantic way, they say, "*Ti amo*." The expression I loved and heard the most was *Ti voglio bene*. This phrase signifies something quite awesome. Translated into English, it means, "I want your good." Learning that Italian phrase brought me back to the love that those youth missionaries had had for me.

Saint Thomas Aquinas, one of the foremost philosophers of the Catholic Church, describes love as willing the good of the other.

This is a love that generously gives of itself, and even greatly sacrifices, to achieve the well-being of another for their own sake. Love's true meaning is to want another's good and to adopt that good as a good for myself.

When I professed my vow of chastity, I had a pretty good idea of what it meant for my love life. Through the vow, I say to the world that as beautiful as the call to marriage is, I was willing to forgo that good for the sake of an even greater good. The vow of chastity asks that I place Jesus as the center of my human love, and I live out my commitment to him in an exclusive way. But the expression of chastity is so much more.

As a youth minister, Ann possessed a generosity and willingness to receive what was in front of her, and she planted a seed of the love that I was made to experience and share through my own vocation. It radically changed my life. But before I could take the next steps, I had to learn how to relate to God in a personal way. I'm still on this journey, but as messy as it can be at times, there is nothing more real than encountering God in the midst of the ups and downs of life. God wants to walk with us, but we have to learn how to walk with him.

Building a Relationship

Having been raised as nominally Catholic, I didn't know what it meant to live a personal relationship with Jesus. For me, religion was about going to Mass, saying prayers, sitting quietly—in other words, being bored. The first clue I received that there was more to relating to God and faith than my own experience was when I actually began to date my big crush.

It turned out that he and I had mutual friends and we began to see one another and get to know one another on weekends. I realized early on that he was a person of faith because he unashamedly attended youth retreats and actively participated when there. I was a bit surprised to find out that while he was Christian, he wasn't a Roman Catholic. He was friends with mostly Catholic kids, which brought him to the youth retreats, but he was Baptist.

One day I awkwardly told him that I really wanted to get to know more about him, so he asked me out on a date. I believe it was during our second date that we began to discuss the differences between our faith traditions. While both Catholics and Baptists worship the same God and share a basic understanding of what it means to be a follower of Jesus, there are differences in the ways that we practice our faith. As a Catholic, I felt we focused on coming together as a community at Mass and participating in the sacraments to receive God's grace. In learning more about the Baptist expression of faith that night, I began to see a new way of relating to God, one that was more personal and less formal. What surprised me most was how deeply this new possibility affected me.

At some point in our conversation I remember him saying,

"I don't know what I would do if I didn't have a relationship with Jesus. We talk all the time."

"You talk to Jesus?"

"Sure. I think my best time with him is when I plow the sugarcane fields for my dad. That's when I listen to music and talk with the Lord."

"Does Jesus talk to you?"

"Yes, he does."

"What does he say?"

I was genuinely intrigued. I had heard older people speak about "talking with the Lord." But I had never heard a sixteen-year-old guy talk about it. For him, prayer was a personal relationship. As much as I wanted to be in a relationship with this gorgeous guy, I found myself wanting to be in a relationship with God even more. I mean, look at how fulfilled it made him feel. I also couldn't ignore the very real desire that lit up inside of me.

When I got home that night, instead of going straight to bed, I made my way back to our spacious living room, knelt down in the darkness of that open space, and asked Jesus to please give me what my crush had. "Lord, I want to know you. I want you to talk to me. Please, teach me how to pray." It was such a simple prayer, but it was a prayer that put a deeply felt desire into words.

This prayer became my own love-language with God. I would whisper it to the Lord whenever I felt that longing rise up in my heart. While it took a long time to even begin to experience God speaking to me, I persisted in asking for God to reveal himself to me in a way that would be real for me.

So, a conversation that I had on a date ended up introducing me to what would become a central element of my daily life: a personal relationship with Jesus. Even now, after many years of living a religious life and attending to daily prayer, I still enter my personal time with Jesus with the humble awareness that prayer is where I seek the face of God in the concrete situations of my life.

No matter how diligently I pursue God's presence in my concrete reality, in many ways I will always be at the beginning. I often get lost in my own ideas and pursuits, wandering away from the constant readiness of heart needed to personally encounter Jesus. But even in my weakness, he promises to send his Holy Spirit to help me. In these moments, I am called to surrender and let the Lord take control. In his way and in his time, he reveals his presence to me.

In the midst of struggle like this, I often reread a letter Mother Teresa wrote to her sisters in which she challenged them to personally encounter Jesus, "one to one." If Jesus is not just an idea but a real living person, then I am also challenged to relate to him that way. Mother Teresa wrote:

"[You] may spend time in chapel—but have you seen with the eyes of your soul how He looks at you with love? Do you really know the living Jesus—not from books, but from being with Him in your heart?"

Her words always move me deeply.

Getting My Attention

After that conversation and my active quest to pray, I began to make different choices, started thinking for myself, and stopped doing whatever my friends were doing just because they were doing it. If this meant staying home, then I stayed home. Regardless of the impetus behind it, this change was a bit earth-shattering for a seventeen-year-old.

One particular Friday, my friends decided to party all weekend, and because I determined to leave those activities behind, I stayed in for the night. Depressed at being home on a Friday night, I began bingeing on Little Debbie oatmeal pies and flipping through the same twenty channels on the TV until I caught the beginning of a movie.

Within seconds I was captivated. The opening scenes were of a monastery, with background music of women chanting.

Whoa! Is this about nuns? And sure enough, the first scene showed nuns. Beautiful nuns looking holy and serene and utterly captivating. I was completely taken in by the imagery and depiction.

The movie was weird, especially to a nominally Catholic girl with very little catechesis. But this is how God works . . . he can use anything he chooses to get our attention. He knew I'd be entranced by the image of nuns, and he was right!

After watching the movie, I found myself longing for God even more. I was fascinated that someone could make such a deep-seated gift of herself to God and dedicate all of her energies toward living and loving in Christ. A nun radically depends on God and his king-ship over her life, confident that everything good ultimately comes from him. She lives life with and in Christ and develops as a person through God's grace. She then spends her life sharing the story of his love for her with others. All of this appealed to me on a deep, mysteri-ous level and I wanted to learn as much as I could about this vocation.

Real-Life Nuns

Soon after watching that movie, I started to attend more faith-based events as "alternative-to-partying" weekend gigs. At one particular retreat, one of the other attendees was Grace, a young woman who was about to enter a convent. I felt this overwhelming urge to con-nect with her. I wanted her to tell me everything she knew about the religious life. During a bit of downtime, I managed to sneak away with this almost-nun to interrogate her on all the gory details of convent life.

What she had to say was interesting and enlightening, but after that conversation, I realized the nun-life was probably not for me. As sweet as this young woman was, I just couldn't see myself happy being docile for the rest of my life (which she seemed to be), nor could I see myself equipped to go down the typical nun career path (which, according to her, was nursing or teaching). I knew I wasn't meek and quiet, I never aspired to be a teacher, nor could I hold it together at the sight of blood. Well, so much for becoming a nun.

About three weeks later, while I was at home one evening, my mom called, "Tracey! Telephone!"

Picking up the receiver, I issued a bored "Hello."

A peppy voice answered, "Hi! This is Olivia! I attended the same retreat you did a few weeks ago. I saw you talking to Grace and thought you might be interested in visiting a convent with me and my family."

"Wait, who are you?"

My whole life was flashing before my very eyes. Who was this person? How did she get my number? And even more to the point, how did she see me talking to Grace?

In my head I was trying to formulate how to say, "No thank you." But I actually heard myself say, "Um, okay."

So the next weekend, I drove with Olivia and her family to the convent of the Daughters of St. Paul in Metairie, Louisiana. Lo and behold, real-life nuns (actually sisters) were right in front of me. I was slightly overwhelmed as I was greeted by these flesh-and-blood sisters who were engaging and talkative. Everything I thought I knew about nuns was put into question. As we sat there, countless thoughts ran through my mind: *These nuns don't even live in a monastery, they work in a bookstore! They're not quiet and prayerful—they're real talkers! They don't wear black and white, but blue! And they drink soda! I thought they were supposed to live on bread and water.*

I was so confused.

But after a few minutes of conversation, I felt that I could calm down. These sisters were real people. Although they dressed alike, they were each unique and had distinct personalities. Even during this first visit, I felt at home. I felt that the sisters welcomed me for who I was and were genuinely interested in getting to know me. I was reminded of that beautiful experience I had had at the retreat. They encouraged visitors to ask questions and they patiently responded to all of our queries—both appropriate and inappropriate. I could picture myself joining them and becoming the person I was called to be with them.

For about two years after, I kept in contact with them, visiting and getting to know more about community life and the Pauline mission. I attended my first year of college and got a job. The sisters encouraged me to keep developing my capacity to pray and to begin learning how to hear from the Lord for myself. As much as they were there to help me discern, I was the only one who could speak to what was in my heart. The time came when I, together with the vocation director, decided that it was time for me to formally continue my discernment by entering the formation program in Boston.

Those first months after entrance were a big mix of excitement and confusion. There were times when I felt I was moving in the right direction and other times when *everything* seemed to be going wrong and I needed to go straight back home. Some of my deepest sufferings came because I believed I had to be someone I was not in order to win God's approval and acceptance.

I'm thankful for the wise spiritual mentors that I had during that time who taught me how to face my own truth before God. I can still remember a meeting I had with my formator, telling her that there was no hope for me making it through postulancy in my current state. She patiently listened to my doubts and fears, and when I was done, she told me that the only way I was going to make it was if I would allow God to reveal himself to me as he really was and not as I was picturing him to be: some weird projection of my own fears.

She held a Bible out to me and said, "You have to get to know the Father for yourself. Nothing I can say can make you understand what I have come to know about him. So, here. Take this Bible and go to him in his Word. Tell him how you really feel and what you really think about him and ask him right then and there to reveal his heart of love for you. He's not afraid of your feelings, he created them. Ask him to show you how he is loving you in all of this mess."

So I did. And I began to see that God really loved me as I was. He showed me that he was faithful to his call. His love for me was greater than any of my failures, weaknesses, or sins. He had been there for me up until that point, so what made me think that suddenly he wouldn't be able to be faithful to me and provide for me in that moment?

On this side of eternity, we never really know God's reasons for permitting certain difficulties and sufferings. We don't get to see the big picture, per se. But prayer helps us to know God, to know his heart, to know that he is a good Father and that he cannot be bad. Having an authentic and personal relationship with God provides the context in which we can trust and surrender to him in the concrete realities we face in life.

Poop Has a Purpose

I remember reading that St. Thomas Aquinas, when dealing with the question of why a good God can permit evil, remarked that the reason was to bring about an even greater good. That's quite a pill to swallow if the suffering ends in physical death. But as Christians, we know that we have both a physical life and a spiritual life. Who is to say that the physical sufferings we endure today may not result in preparing us for the life of eternity?

My own perspective on this very question, as a young professed sister, was enlightened one day. As media nuns, we tend to be early adapters when it comes to technology. Right after my First Profession of vows, all of our communities received community email addresses. If anyone wanted to send a sister an email, they had to send it to the community email address. At supper we would have "mail call," during which one of the sisters logged on to the internet and retrieved all the emails for the sisters in the community. She would print them out and distribute them around suppertime.

Every now and then, my mom or dad would send me an email. They are both Cajuns from south Louisiana, so their first language is Cajun French. Both of my parents use many French words as terms of endearment. One of my dad's favorites for me is *poupée*, which translates to "doll" in English.

Now, my father also had a tendency to cut words in half. It's more economical, I guess. At work, Dad had renamed most of his buddies "Podnah," which then became simply "Pod." When it came to him speaking sweetly to me, he just called me "Poup." He pronounced it something like "Pup." But not quite.

One evening, another sister was sorting through the emails.

"Sister Theresa."

"Sister Marie."

Pause.

She confusedly looked around the room. "Who's Poop?"

Did I mention, Dad's not much of a speller?

My fellow sisters all looked at me then, their expressions ranging from astounded to curious. I smiled to let them know it was okay. From all the visible evidence, it looked like Dad called me "Poop." It looks bad. It sounds bad. But not for me. Despite what appears on the surface: I know my dad. I know his heart. He's a good dad. He just can't spell.

There are realities we live through that make us question God's goodness and promises to us. Some sufferings make us question his Word and his fidelity. Some things are so traumatic and painful that the idea of receiving reality as it is just feels like masochism. 'Surrender,' 'acceptance,' and 'receptivity' are words I don't want to hear during times like that. In these times, I would much rather be elsewhere, anywhere other than where I am. Sometimes things in life are so hard that it feels as though God is handing us a letter that begins "Dear Poop." It's times like this that we can really question the Father's love for us.

During a dark period, Saint Teresa of Ávila famously said to the Lord, "If this is how you treat your friends, no wonder you have so few." Sometimes you can't help but feel she was right.

But life has taught me the hard lesson that sometimes the only way to really grow and bear good fruit in the world is through suffering and difficulty. A friend of mine always reminds me when I'm complaining about being in a hard place, "You know that the best fertilizer is actually poop, right?"

Yeah, I know. Poop has a purpose.

What I'm Living

Authentically living and sharing from my real experience has been and continues to be a constant challenge to me. I know that my witness to Christ has to come out of what I am actually living with the Lord. I can often hear George's plea for me to never be content to hand out leftovers but to draw from the daily relationship I have with God.

Receiving what I'm living is the first step to how I meet the Lord. If God is a good Father, then I know that whatever his providence permits is a place of encounter. It can also be a place of nourishment for others. While God never wills suffering, his grace may permit it so that he can bring about an even greater good.

Through our media mission, I carry my relationship with God into the world and show by my witness what it means to be a disciple. Being called to witness the love of God extends to every aspect of who I am and where I live, especially social media. While many aspects of social media can distract me from true encounters with God, myself, and others, much can be said for the many ways social media can be utilized as a means for authentic witness. What better way to tell the story of how I am trying to remain with Jesus in the insanity that is 2020 than through a daily post? Social media is a great platform for this kind of witness.

My social media presence on Instagram began as an offshoot of my presence on Facebook. Whatever I posted on Facebook was re-posted on Instagram until the day I received a beautiful, handwritten note in the mail. The sender had taken the time and effort to letter my name and address beautifully on the envelope. Seeing this note reminded me of the attraction I have always had for making beautiful letters. As an artist, I had worked in typography, digital design, and drawing, but I'd never dedicated myself to learning how to letter.

Instagram became my lettering school. I studied the letters of other artists I followed and gradually started to letter meaningful quotes, phrases, and words. It took time and lots of practice to finally begin to have an ease and flow in my creations. I renamed my account to @sistah_tee_letters and post my art with a spiritual application of God's Word in my life.

Posting my lettering keeps me faithful to the challenge to receive what I'm being given. Depending on my own capacity to know my own heart and bring it into relationship with God and his Word, I am able to express how those two realities meet in real life. Instagram is where I tell the story of how I'm trying to remain with the Lord. It's a reflection of my discipleship, how I daily try to show up to God's truth about my reality and use my art to share what my prayer shows me. I'm giving what I'm living. No leftovers.

When I am lettering, I usually start by asking the Lord, "How are you with me right here? Right now?" Maybe I'm living something hard at the moment and I want to run away from it. I pray for God's grace to be the light that shows me how he is with me. Then I pick up the Word of God, usually a passage from that day's liturgy, and I ask to see my reality through the merciful eyes of Jesus.

And then I wait. And watch. And listen.

I go wherever my prayer takes me and I ask God to allow his Word to be done in my life, as it was in Mary's life. "Be it done to me as you say, Lord." I open myself in receptivity. Sometimes I feel God speaks through the Scripture; other times an image or memory appears. I've learned to talk to the Lord about all of it and be attentive to how he may be revealing his heart of love for me.

A Beautiful Writer

Receiving what I'm living calls me to open my heart to discovering God's presence in whatever comes my way. It means receiving the present moment in all of its beauty and promise as well as in its pain and difficulty. It means accepting the Lord's call in the midst of my reality and allowing it to draw me forth on my journey toward him. Sometimes God's call fills me with hope and enthusiasm and I am given the energy and courage to step into the unknown to do the best I can with the resources I have. Other times I am not so courageous. Sometimes the call of God reveals my own great limits and incapacities and I feel far, far away from fulfilling God's plan for me.

When the words "You're a beautiful writer" were spoken over me by a very nice, praying man, I did not take the time to consider them as true prophetic words. In my estimation, they were simply a mistake.

Writing is not easy for me. It's a struggle. I have to work hard at it and I often want to quit. But when I think of the biblical understanding of prophesy, I remember that a prophetic Word is a gift given by God. This gift is given to advance the spiritual welfare of the person to whom it is spoken. It is spoken to encourage, to build up. Because that Word is inspired by God's spirit, it has the power to activate and energize the gift within the one to whom it is given.

The question is, can I trust that God has a good purpose for me, even through this difficulty?

1 TIMOTHY 1:18-19

In his first letter to Timothy, St. Paul encourages Timothy to use the prophesies spoken over him as weapons as he engages in spiritual warfare by faith. And it is a battle! Think about it. When we hear ourselves speaking in absolutes like *I'll never be able to finish this! I can't! It's impossible!* we can be sure that this is not a movement of the good spirit. The Spirit of God moves in peace, in hope, in love, and in truth.

In many ways, being a "beautiful writer" is a call from the Lord to me. It is a glimpse of the way the Father sees me. Seeing as I do that I do not have the inner natural resources to fulfill this identity, it can be easy to fall into a spiritual sadness and hopelessness and give up. But the battle needs to be fought! To put up a fight with the spirit of paralysis and fear is to exercise hope. And hope is best expressed through prayer. Prayer manifests in words, the desire for God to create what we cannot create of ourselves. This is the best way to bridge the gap between God's call and my limited reality. First, I receive my truth as it is and admit that I am weak and incapable. Then I simply turn to the Lord in utter trust and beg him for the grace to do what I cannot do on my own.

In the convent, we pray a very simple prayer quite often throughout the day because it states the heart of the matter: "By myself I can do nothing, but with God I can do all things."

Yes, with God all things are possible. Even writing this essay.

DON'T RUN
FROM THE
MESSINESS

SR. DANIELLE VICTORIA LUSSIER, FSP

When I was an infant, my maternal grandmother, Nancy, called me her "buddah baby." She would set me in the middle of a blanket and leave me there, content for hours, and never worry whether I would wander. Fast-forward twenty-eight years to breakfast at our local Big Boy. I am with my paternal grandmother, Julia, and my cousin, who asks her what she thinks about me becoming a "nun." No doubt skeptical whether I could remain in one place for any length of time, let alone a convent, Julia stuck her fork into a short stack of buttery pancakes and, with an eyebrow raised, replied, "I'll believe it when I see it!" Both of my grandmothers knew me well. God, the master artist of my life, knows me best.

The Paradox of Stillness and Activity Is What First Attracted Me to the Daughters of Saint Paul

To live with an interior monastic silence and recollection while simultaneously being in the center of culture, media, and mainstream life seemed gritty yet serene. As sisters, we call ourselves "contemplatives in action." I must admit, when I first heard that phrase, I imagined becoming a nun was more like being initiated into the ancient tradition of samurai warriors or becoming Jedi for Jesus than setting on a path to becoming Sister Mary Pious of the Ever Quiet and Weaned Baby Jesus.

Every religious order has a special devotion to a specific title of Jesus, Mary, and particular saints. As someone who returned to religion after college, I was excited and overwhelmed learning all the different devotions and titles attributed to Jesus and Mary. For the Daughters, Jesus is Divine Master and Mary is Queen of Apostles. These titles were intimidating as they suggested an all-encompassing pedagogy and mentorship in the way of the spiritual life: Christ as our Master Teacher is the Truth for our mind, the Way for our will, and the Life that forms our heart. Mary, as the First Apostle, having formed Christ in her womb, is our nurturer and multiplier of fruitfulness as Christ is formed in us.

Through St. Paul, our order's Father and founder, my own humanity finds a place amid the epic holiness of Jesus and Mary. In life, Paul was a force to be reckoned with, a bold follower of

God. He was an outsider who considered himself the least of the Apostles because he persecuted the first Christians. Unlike "The Twelve," he wasn't taught the faith by journeying with Jesus over time. Rather, he encountered Christ on a zealous pursuit from Jerusalem to Damascus with a government-issued mandate to seek out and arrest followers of "The Way." Ultimately, the intent was to return them to Jerusalem for questioning and execution. He had big plans. God had bigger plans. Instead Paul was knocked down, blinded and humbled by the light of Christ. That encounter with Christ, who Paul understood in that moment to be present in the people he was persecuting, radically changed the trajectory of Paul's life. Realizing that the God he had dedicated his life to serving as a faithful Jew was also the One he was persecuting wrecked Paul's heart and radically changed his life. From that moment, his life had a new trajectory and stark clarity of focus: to communicate to others, however he could, through whatever means possible, the glory of the living Lord and his love for everyone. Even in prison, he was writing and teaching and sharing his love for Christ and his friends, winning the hearts and minds of the guards assigned to him. Paul was a big personality, relentless in his pursuit of truth; he loved magnanimously and he suffered with courage.

What I love most about Paul, though, is that he boasted of his weaknesses. He was shipwrecked, beaten, stoned, ignored, mocked, rejected, held captive, chased out of towns to the point of having to be lowered over a wall in a basket to escape death, and was eventually beheaded for his love of Christ. Paul's life was messy, but he wasn't alone in the mess and he knew it. Paul's strength was his weakness, because it was there that Christ was able to enter his life and work miracles through him. The more Paul suffered, the more intimately he allowed Christ to enter the mess of his life. Christ's loving presence not only sustained him through all his suffering, but made his efforts bear much fruit for others even until today.

Saint Paul's life is made ever more fruitful centuries later when, as consecrated women, the Daughters of Paul sit in silence and prayer. In our daily activity we are in solidarity with the working world, with all its demands and pressures, affecting family and community life. This is precisely why our prayer is to be a conversation of deep listening and sharing honestly with Jesus. Like Paul, to the degree that we enter into the realness of this relationship, our lives are filled with a fruitfulness that calls us out of ourselves and into the world to share him with others. As religious sisters, we are called to bring *all of ourselves* to Christ—the good, the broken, the ugly, the beautiful, our weaknesses, joys, and gifts. All of who we are. We are also called to bring all of *you* (yes, you, the person who picked up this book). As daughters of St. Paul, we inherit Paul's heart, which we know to be one and the same with Christ's heart. His is a heart that is burning for you. To be Pauline is to desire that everyone reading these pages and everyone you love know that fierce and very real love of Jesus. I pray that you know how tenderly and relentlessly he loves you and is with you, in all that you are and all that you face each day. He wants to reveal your deepest and truest self to you so that you can become a clear communication of his unique love for humanity.

After all, who doesn't sometimes desire silence amid our busy world? Who doesn't want activity filled with meaning and purpose? These are lovely bookends to uphold the ideal, but the stuff in between, the actual journey to being honest with yourself and with God, is where the realness of life is felt. It's also in this in-between where the beauty of living totally devoted to God is discovered and authenticated. And it's messy. If I'm going to be real with you, I have to admit that it's tempting to want to run from that messiness. It's been tempting to me before and I have no doubt that it will also be tempting to me in the future. It's tempting, because it is precisely in the very "stuff" of our lives that the authenticity and beauty we seek is with us in "it"— whatever the "it" may be. It's scary to face that "it," but only in facing it can you truly find an enduring peace that comes from knowing that your identity at its core is rooted in a God and Father who loves you. He delights in all that you are, right where you are. He is ever present, laboring for your good amid the mess. He loves you enough to enter into the "stuff" of your life and he loves you so much more that he won't allow you to stay there. His love is creative and re-creative. God brought order out of chaos, beauty out of ugliness, and life from death, and he invites us with our every breath to co-create with him in our daily lives. He is crafting your life into a masterpiece.

I pray my story offers hope amid that temptation and courage to dare to see the gift that awaits you in the messiness when we choose to live it in Christ. Do not be afraid, he is with you in it.

I Have Chased After Beauty and Authenticity All My Life

But like Paul, my life changed radically when I discovered that these formerly nebulous concepts that I had been looking for were really a "Who." To put it more distinctly, a Who has a face and is a Person with a capital *P*. This entire shift in my perspective happened when I realized as a young adult that this person, namely Jesus, had been with me in the messiness of my life all along. More importantly, he had been with me most intimately throughout the rougher periods of my life, the very same periods when I had thought him irrelevant and completely absent.

Before I jump to that moment, I want to paint a picture for you of my upbringing, mainly what my relationship with and understanding of God was like growing up in my family. Often people who ask me how or when I knew I wanted to become a sister assume that I came out of the womb as baby Sister Danielle, prepped, ready, and shouting, "Here I am, Lord!" It definitely wasn't that clean-cut for me.

My parents married young; my mother was seventeen and my father nineteen. They had both been raised Catholic and later decided together to join the then-blossoming Catholic charismatic movement in Michigan. Like a breath of new life in the Church, the charismatic movement focused on becoming alive in the gifts of the Holy Spirit, delving into Scripture, and encountering Jesus in a personal and living way. I remember attending Mass in a school gymnasium as a young child with my family. My father, with one hand raised and another resting me against his chest, while I listened to his deep, reverberating voice join the waves of indistinguishable sounds of praise speaking and singing in tongues. My parents were young, fervent, and had big dreams for themselves and their growing family. They had high hopes of raising their children to feel the same passion and zeal that stirred in their hearts. And every step of the way they entrusted their children and their path to God.

They began building their family right away, having nine children and suffering one miscarriage by the time my mother was thirty-three. I was the seventh born, preceded by Caty and followed by Loretta, who was the eighth child, while Marie came last, but not least, more like a cherry on top because of her spunk; the baby of our big ol' Catholic family. One of my earliest memories goes back to when I was just three years old. My mother was pregnant with Loretta. In my memory, I am standing in my crib flanked by two sets of bunk beds, surrounded by my siblings. The house we lived in was an 850-square-foot, one-level bungalow with a cement-block basement. "We used every inch of that house," my mother reminded me recently. My father said, "We used the dining room as our bedroom. It was the first home we owned, and though we couldn't afford anything larger, we felt it was God providing for our family and an answer to prayer."

Although there was a lot of joy and laughter in our house as I was growing up, these were also tumultuous years. Over the course of almost as many years, our family moved eleven times, as my parents struggled through the discoveries of their own limitations. Before I was born, my father was in the air force and went to school for his degree while raising my older siblings. He worked multiple jobs to support our growing family and my mother stayed home, keeping an immaculate house while caring for all of us. Though my parents had started their family with a faithful fervor and a vibrant sense of community, over time our family practice of the Catholic faith slowly waned until it was mostly nonexistent. Although we weren't going to church any longer, we did continue to rely on God's care and providence. It was a confusing time for me. During my most formative years, I often felt that I had been left to navigate and figure out life on my own.

One day, in a desperate desire for order amid what felt like chaos, I was inspired to clear out a corner of the basement to make it into my own artist's studio. For Christmas that year my parents bought me a set of glass paints. I used them to paint on stored furniture from the previous houses we lived in. I poured all the pent-up frustration, anger, and heaviness I felt into creating something simple and beautiful. Bright fish and underwater scenes detailed formerly blank glass vases that had been strewn across the room. Stacked appliances like our vintage metal toaster, napkin holder, and tissue-box cover were striped and polka-dotted in vibrant patterns, marking a safe place to pour out my heart. More importantly, in this safe haven, I had a real sense of God's presence, and I could openly talk to the Lord about what was on my heart. The bright colors and whimsical scenes introduced something beautiful amid the messiness of my life in that moment and allowed me to connect to something greater than myself.

Even in My Earliest Memories, My Desire to Be an Artist Was Strong

I inherited my artistic ability from both my parents, and my mother fostered my creativity in a particular way. Before marrying my father, she worked in her small town painting trucks, signs, and ads for some extra money, embarking on a promising career as a commercial artist. But once she started her family, she chose to focus on raising her children full-time. Although she gave up an artistic career, my childhood was threaded with creativity, crafts, and play made extraordinary through the simplest of means. Having inherited her imaginative spirit and impressed by how she poured her creativity into raising her children, I always imagined myself having a big family of my own and being an artist at the same time. My mother would gather the odds and ends of my father's woodworking projects and show us how to turn the block into anything we wanted. We would paint all over it and glue various knickknacks

on it, then she would turn it into a garden scene or a scene of balloons in the sky. She had a way of taking whatever was there and making a story out of it. If I was discouraged because something I was working on wasn't turning out the way I imagined, she would extend a stem from the base of a blotch of paint, effortlessly brush two leaves, and define the lines of the petals saying, "See, there was a flower in there waiting to come out."

I also absolutely adored my siblings. When we fought, we would be pretty merciless with each other, but when it came to being creative and collaborating, we could turn backyard play into a scene enchanting enough to rival an HGTV reality show. One winter, I remember building a two-story igloo off the side of the house. It took days, and my siblings and I all had a part in the construction. Before it began to melt, we served hot cocoa and entered the multilevel structure through our bedroom windows. It was magical.

It's impressive to me now as an adult to reflect on these memories. There were so many of these simple joy-filled moments with my family, and though they are precious to me now, I have to admit they were not the most potent for me growing up. There were times I didn't feel the safety of the structures in my family's life. When things began to crumble for my parents, life for my siblings and me became unsure, insecure, and scary. With Swiss-cheese-sized holes in my understanding of the faith and no faith community to turn to, these were the moments that sowed seeds of doubt regarding God's love for me. Questions about love, family, and identity grew like weeds among wheat. How can there be joy in the suffering?

How can there be security despite the insecurity? How can there be creativity and new life though we seem to lack so much? These questions were like a tapestry weaving together the simple and the complex, the light and the dark, the joy amid suffering, as well as love and disappointment into an image I couldn't make sense of at the time. All of these contradictions that I felt in my life came out in my art. Over and over again the theme of a mangled and disfigured face reappeared in whatever medium I took up.

I spent the next six years trying to use my gifts in the arts to draw, paint, photograph, film, and poeticize my way to a clearer image. Life seemed full of contradictions. My journey pursuing these questions through art would later teach me that these paradoxes are signs of God's mystery and presence. The mangled image resembles Christ's face crowned with thorns and wrapped by the ugliness of sin. Life can look a lot like Good Friday sometimes. For a long time I sat in the shadow of the Cross, but the beauty of the Cross comes with the rising of the Son on Easter Sunday. True beauty doesn't shy away from the ugliness of life and it doesn't neglect to tell the full truth of the redemption that awaits us on the other side of the darkness. Pope Emeritus Benedict XVI wrote, "Art and the saints are the best apologetics."

It seems to me that beautiful art and a beautiful life are the best defense or proof of the truth. Throughout my formative years, I wrestled with beauty through art and seeking answers about whether or not I could truly live a beautiful life. Beauty in art and beauty in a virtuous life are the evidence that truth and goodness are real and attainable. Having a beautiful life calls us to live more authentically. The good example of another evokes a response within us and speaks to our dignity, inviting us to become more of what we were made for. A beautiful work of art can captivate our senses and call us out of ourselves into the mystery of things beyond our intellect. And a beautiful work of art includes both light and dark, light and shadows. When these elements come together in harmony, they allude to the fuller story. True beauty seeks to make visible the invisible. And so art became the only sacred space I trusted to seek deeper understanding for my life.

When I received a scholarship to attend the Rhode Island School of Design, I felt like I was truly living my dreams. And so art and delving into the creative process became the center of my life in college. Spending hours a day developing my gifts and discussing the deepest ponderings of my heart with others was exciting and stimulating. But with the constant activity, I barely noticed how God and faith were slowly being worked out of my daily conversations. Without realizing it, I had wrapped my identity solely around being an artist. My art and the process of creating for me became a visual deconstruction of the family values, beliefs, and perceptions of love that I grew up with and witnessed. I documented my family over a six-year span, photographing the "artifacts" of our family life. I filmed the spaces we grew up in, creating installation art that provided an experience of the emotional landscape I had experienced as a child. One example of a piece I created with my parents was titled *The Conversation You Never Have That I Wish You'd Have.* I recorded an interview with both of them over the phone, asking each of them a series of questions regarding their relationship. I then cut my voice out and spliced their voices together. The result was a gut-wrenching audio track of two people talking at each other about their most painful experiences of the other. I still look back on these years of my artistic search for meaning with heartache over some of the ways I explored our family pain. But what I didn't know then and can see now is the way grace would manifest itself in and through my family in a way that changed my life.

I desperately desired to make sense of the disunity and messiness, but only felt more disintegrated as I continued in my work. Pursuing meaning in suffering solely through my art left me empty. I realize now that I wasn't able to integrate my joys and sorrows and the contradictions I felt in my life without God. Eventually, I felt I needed to step back from my own experience and broaden my questioning. This brought me to documentary filmmaking.

By this time I was disillusioned about love and didn't believe that anything outside of self-interest could bring two people together. My work remained autobiographical in that I was still seeking answers about the nature of love, but now it was with other people's stories. I finished my senior year by making a film about the dependents of deployed soldiers in Germany. I followed several couples and their families over the course of a year, detailing the effects of deployment and frontline combat on their marriages and family life. Though I did meet couples in situations that confirmed my doubts about love, I also encountered heroic efforts by husbands and wives to hold a place for their spouse away in combat. When some returned with PTSD, I witnessed couples begin to journey together through it. A shared faith and relationship with Jesus made all the difference in those cases. It was in documenting these lives that I began to feel the responsibility of being entrusted with the retelling of their stories. This sense of responsibility was an invitation for me to reflect more deeply beyond my anger and the disillusionment that colored my assumptions about their lives and my own. Documenting the devotion of these couples in the face of so much suffering and mystery began to open my heart to seeing my parents and their love through the lens of sacrifice and faithfulness. This was the beginning of something new for me. Like these couples in my film, my parents didn't run from each other's messiness. They weren't perfect, but they stayed together and strove to love each other as best they could amid the messiness. My senior-year show was composed of a showing of the documentary I produced from this time titled *Dependents of Deployed Soldiers* and a display of photographs from my time on the base. My parents, Grandmother Nancy, and five of my siblings and their children came. I didn't realize it at the time, but I scheduled my show on Good Friday. On Holy Saturday, the next day, I dropped them off at the airport so they could celebrate Easter with the rest of the family in Michigan.

Months Later after College Graduation, I Had a Conversion Experience That Radically Changed My Life

I was dating someone at the time, and our relationship was becoming more serious. He was an atheist and I had strayed far enough from the practice of my faith that it didn't really matter much to me. I was surrounded by people and experiences that didn't seem congruent with my Catholic upbringing and I was learning about the greater world.

One of the reasons I was drawn to my boyfriend was that he seemed to approach life with a sober honesty that I found refreshing. I saw myself relating to him as I struggled to integrate my new life and my Catholic upbringing. Like the repulsion of two magnetic forces, much of the time interiorly I felt like I was being pulled apart. On one hand, I had a nostalgic love for the Mass and the solemn festivity of my Catholic upbringing. I also really desired to live the ideal that was presented to me through what I understood of the teachings of the Church, especially regarding chastity, which increasingly felt like an impossible ideal. On the other hand, I had my art, friends, and desire for social justice. At the time, I was unfamiliar with Catholic social teaching and didn't have a solid understanding of Christian anthropology. All I knew was that I didn't see my current life fitting in with my experience of the Church.

The experience of falling in love brought me to a place of decisiveness. I decided I needed to let go of my faith in order to be free of the tension it caused in my life and to pursue a future with this person I loved. After coming to that conclusion, I felt lighter, unburdened of a weight that had been consuming me. I was nervously excited to share my decision with my boyfriend. We had planned to meet up at his house. Arriving, I rang the doorbell, filled with joy to tell him that I loved him and that I wanted our relationship to be more serious. I couldn't hold it in any longer.

After some conversation, I led into telling him I had something that I wanted to say to him. I barely remember what we spoke about or at what point exactly I said it, just that I took a deep breath. I began to exhale the words "I love you." In that moment, looking into my boyfriend's eyes, I knew that God had a different plan for me. Without a shadow of a doubt, I knew three things to be true: that God was real, that I did not know him, and that the previous conclusions I had come to about who God is and the influence that he had in my life were wrong. I was wrong about the way I had thought I had "figured" out how to see the world.

This life-changing moment was simultaneously extraordinarily freeing and immensely devastating. It was liberating in that I had this concrete sense that I didn't have to figure out an identity for myself anymore. I knew that God was real, and that he had a plan for my life and an intention for my existence that I didn't have to come up with on my own. And it was shattering, because the carpet had been pulled out from underneath my life.

While this tremendous shift was happening inside me, I was both laughing and crying, and understandably, my boyfriend was confused. I let him know that I had wanted to tell him that I loved him but that something just happened, that I needed to go home, and I would call him later. He was sympathetic, assuring me that it was a beautiful thing to say and that he would give me whatever time I needed.

I went home and called one of my sisters, whom I hadn't spoken honestly to in a long time. When she answered the phone, I poured my heart out, sharing everything in my life—what I had been thinking, how I had been living, and what had just happened. Then I said, "Now, I am going to be quiet and I need you to speak truth to me." She only very simply and calmly said, "Danielle, you have always sought truth, you know what you need to do. Do it."

We got off the phone and I decided to fly home the next day. After all the searching for meaning and peace from the pain I felt in my childhood, my first impulse was to return home. I could feel and trust my family's love for me for the first time and I just wanted to be close to them. It felt like backlogged grace that was waiting for me all along—for the moment I could receive it. I stayed there a week. I am still amazed by the warmth and generosity my siblings and my parents showed in receiving me. Each sat down with me, and we talked about everything that had been going on in my life. They all listened at length, asked meaningful questions, and we discussed the crossroads I was at. I had never felt so loved. Later a spiritual director would say to me that "A family is only as strong as the difficult conversations they can have." After this experience I knew the kind of "stuff" my family was made of. It came from the courage and perseverance of my parents, who relentlessly never gave up on each other. That "stuff" was the face of love. At the end of the week, I knew what I needed to do next, but I was hesitant to move forward. I was still deeply invested and attached to the life I had been crafting. I had built my identity on a road map for a life that I no longer wanted. It was incredibly unsettling.

Though the attachment to my plans and the pain of letting them go lasted a while after the conversion experience, my ambition for crafting a future for myself was redirected toward a deep thirst to know God. The night before I flew back to Rhode Island, I met up with a friend, Therese. She took me to a local pub, and over a pitcher of beer, she asked me to tell her what happened. So I shared with her what I had experienced, recounting all my actions and the emotions surrounding my conversion. When I ended, she looked at me with such conviction and proclaimed, "That was Jesus! Danielle, you encountered Jesus." And I knew that she was right. She had called out and given voice to what I was hesitant to claim. I began to cry. It became clear that I needed to move home, and soon, so I could be surrounded by people who would support my life's new path. I didn't want to take the chance that I would go back to my old life and not follow this grace. When I returned to Rhode Island, I shared everything with my boyfriend and we broke things off. It was heart-wrenching. I spent the next three days packing and hurrying about to distract myself from the tremendous ache in my chest. I was grateful it rained most of those three days because the rain hid my tears.

After I moved home, my time was composed of devouring the

Word of God in Scripture and in the lives of the saints during the day, and waitressing at night to pay back my student loans. During my first six months back, I would get home late at night after work and watch *The Passion of the Christ*, directed by Mel Gibson. The suffering of Christ depicted in that movie met me in the pain I was experiencing. It was a time of mourning and thanksgiving. In the beginning months, my ex-boyfriend called every so often to check in and to see if I would be coming back. The last time he called, he seemed to know my decision and we said our goodbyes. We haven't spoken since. I still pray for him and want nothing for him but the best.

Placing My Identity as an Artist on the Altar

In the aftermath of my conversion, every time I went to pick up my camera, I picked up that ten-year plan. It was like I was picking up everything that I had been freed from in that moment when I met the Lord. I could feel the weight of it, the heft of the life path that I had left behind. In lifting that lens, I remembered all of the strain that came with thinking that I had to decide everything. In college, I had everything I had ever dreamed of. I was in control of my life, but I also felt so alone and felt an immense amount of pressure to craft something magnificent of my life. And I was lonely, and the pressure was crushing me. Behind the ambition and the hard work, I was feverishly seeking a way to be free from having to prove myself and to just be. Being an artist gave me a place in the world and armed me with a way to make sense of the things that were mysterious or painful in life. I had found new meaning in the mystery of Christ's life, death, and resurrection. Yet every time I picked up my camera I was picking up that plan to set myself free. I decided nothing was worth sacrificing the peace that I had found. So I placed all my gifts in the arts on the altar and told God, "Hand this back to me when I can use it for your glory alone."

The Lord did provide moments to live the experience of picking up my camera differently. The restaurant where I waitressed was a Mongolian-themed barbecue that benefited a not-for-profit in Mongolia that helped support local youth. Once, when I was having a conversation with the owner, I offered to make a short film about how this business endeavor impacted the lives of the Mongolian youth, as I was moved by the fact that this business was looking to do good for others halfway across the world. In the spirit of adventure and a generous desire to highlight the good, the owner sent me and a friend to Mongolia for five weeks to make this film.

I spent much of my time in Mongolia photographing Soviet cement buildings painted in bright Mongolian colors. My photos told the story of a people who were reclaiming a space that had been imposed upon, and their vibrant lead-painted stairways, murals, and homes spoke of a culture that was seeking to express its own identity amid the Communist art and architecture that had occupied their territory for so long. In a small way I was reminded of the little corner of my basement where I attempted to carve out a safe place for myself amid cement blocks and a tumultuous history.

While I was there, I visited the single Catholic church in the capital of Ulaanbaatar. It was the cathedral, shaped in the form of a Mongolian home called a *ger* or a yurt. While looking out from the cathedral rooftop, I was astounded at the thousands of small plots of land where patched-together homes were packed side by side, and at the vibrancy that this country contained. My days had been consumed with learning local people's stories, with becoming immersed in the culture. On the cathedral rooftop I had a profound feeling of belonging to people like the ones I had met and I desired to share their stories. My heart expanded with the desire to bring healing to the world through my art.

After That Trip to Mongolia, I Felt the Distinct Invitation to Leave Everything to Do This, to Devote Myself Entirely to This

But at the time, I didn't have a clear understanding of what "vocation" meant. I thought of it in the dictionary sense as a job or a career. It wasn't until several years later while I was on a retreat that I learned that a vocation was more than a career—that it was firmly rooted in identity. A vocation is not so much about what I am called to do as it is about who I was made to be.

When I got back from Mongolia, I was invited to attend several retreats. These various retreats provided some insight, but it was on a thirty-day silent retreat that I had a moment of clarity in prayer. It was like a drawstring pulling together the bag that held all these memories from my childhood and while growing up, moments when I wasn't pursuing my faith and Christ felt really far. This time, I felt he had been with me through it all. I felt like my heart was already spoken for and I needed to pursue my relationship with Jesus, to become totally his and serve those who he would put in my life. Although I could have never imagined it before then, I knew my heart had belonged to Christ from the beginning. The Lord was making it clear that not only was I called to a consecrated life, but that he desired for me to use my artistic gifts in my calling. I distinctly remember in prayer that I knew I didn't want to paint statues and icons but that through my art, I wanted to tell the deepest stories of people's hearts and to share the beauty of their lives. I wanted to be a storyteller.

And so, in that same prayer, I remember telling him, "Lord, I want to communicate you and your story to the world through my art."

He answered my prayer several days later, when two sisters dressed in blue showed up at the retreat house. There was a lunch at which all members of the retreat were able to speak to one another, and at which the sisters shared their mission of communicating Christ through all forms of media. Here were nuns who operated cameras in their film and recording studios. I was captivated by how they spoke about their spirituality. The sisters shared that they pray before the Blessed Sacrament, bringing all of who they are to the Lord, and that through that encounter, God speaks to their real life, and they are transformed. They then share the fruit of their prayer through art that they create, the books that they write, the music they record, and the stories that they tell. Seeing these sisters talk and pray, I was attracted to their authenticity. They radiated joy. The sacrifice of their entire lives and creativity to God seemed to bring out the uniqueness of who they are rather than squelching or homogenizing their personalities. I could see that they themselves became the "medium" or the canvas. In their genuine goodness and humanity each sister is a communication of God. Their mission and their life spoke to me. I felt called to become a Daughter of St. Paul.

One of the sisters invited me to visit their motherhouse at the end of my retreat, and so I spent the last two days of my retreat there. I knew immediately that this was where I was supposed to be. I didn't have an overwhelming feeling of elation or joy, but I knew that my presence there was God's will and that this was where, through living the life of these sisters, I would heal and grow and integrate my creativity—the gifts I had placed on the altar for the Lord.

Seven years later, my parents, along with eight of my siblings and their families (including thirty of my nieces and nephews) flew into Boston to witness my First Profession of vows. It was the happiest day of my life and a miracle of grace to be surrounded by my family that had loved me so profoundly into this moment. My parents and I wept as we processed with our arms interlocked down the aisle. I held my burning baptismal candle out in front of me. The symbolism was not lost on us. My parents were offering me, the fruit of their love, to God. My baptismal candle was symbolic of the light of faith that my parents passed on to me and their parents had passed on to them. That light of faith was bearing new life as I professed vows of chastity, poverty, and obedience. This is done in the middle of the Mass, at the same moment in a Catholic wedding when the bride and groom exchange vows with one another. With my hand over my heart as I professed my vows, I experienced the Lord saying to me that he was giving back my offering from long ago. I had placed my gifts on the altar in an act of surrender in trust and love. In return, he gave me a clear and beautiful way to glorify him as a consecrated religious who is specifically called to communicate his message of redemption and the greatest love story of all time: *his*. I had given him my previous life, and in return he had gifted me with my most authentic life—the opportunity to live out of the core of who I really am. Jesus Christ entered our sin and death so that in him we might glorify God with our life. In him we are a new creation; the old has passed away and he promises that as we surrender our lives to him, he will become the context for our life. He will be our meaning in the suffering and mystery. He is faithful to his promises. As I know him, I get to know myself. Every day at Mass I place myself in this truth as I prepare to receive Jesus in the Eucharist at Communion. I say a daily prayer renewing my vows, centering my identity and the fruitfulness of my activity that day in being totally his, giving glory to God and peace to humanity.

Not all are called to be an artist in the literal sense, but all are called to make a masterpiece of their life.

—Blessed John Paul II

I have come to see the discovery of beauty amid suffering, in my own life and the lives of others, as my own artistic process, which is gradually evolving as my relationship with Christ deepens. When we don't see our weakness as a gift, we run from the messiness of our human experience and compensate by making our work saccharine, sterile, inauthentic, and devoid of the life and depth that re-creation imbues. God is with you in the messiness. He is re-creating in and through you in the messiness. Good and true art needs to be lived with God. It is re-creative love that makes art and life truly beautiful. Stick around and together you will make beautiful things. He will make a masterpiece with your life.

EVERY BIT *of* YOUR LIFE IS SACRED ENOUGH *to* PROCLAIM CHRIST *to* OUR
#MEDIAWORLD

SR. JACQUELINE JEAN-MARIE GITONGA, FSP

I n the modern, constantly moving world, God can sometimes seem far away—a distant being or a spirit up in the skies somewhere who left the scene of our daily reality aeons ago. Even for devout Christians, especially when we are going through tough times, God can seem essentially nonexistent. One might even feel that this God is someone whom we need to "appease" with trinkets like good deeds and impeccable behavior, so that we can *feel* accepted and heard. Even the most faithful ponder how to be committed and connected to a good and loving God in a world so full of incomprehensible problems, complex situations, violence and injustices, and racing technological advances. To stay faithful today can feel like living a dichotomized life, one that is preposterous, or "too idealistic," or out of touch with reality. In fact, one might find living according to the Christian Gospel too "rigorous" an existence, a lifestyle that is too strict and "no fun." Many can see following God faithfully as effectively burying your head in the sand.

For the religious like myself, that mind-set couldn't be further from the truth. Having a vibrant relationship with God depends on one factor, one verb that changes everything: "encounter." I can tell you from personal experience that when you personally encounter this kind, merciful, loving, personal *Christian* God, *everything* changes for the better. To walk this journey called life with Him may not be an easy road (and it often doesn't matter what path you take in this life), but if you are called to the religious life, it is possible, quite fulfilling, and definitely worth it. Yes, I know that following God might make me stand out like a sore thumb in some circles, but I ask myself: *What kind of life would you like to live that makes a difference? What kind of legacy would you want to leave behind?* I know my answer.

My life is thus a testimony to the reality that you can be both a faithful Christian and an active participant in this world. Growing up, I certainly never imagined that I would be where I am today: a Catholic religious sister, a missionary, a consecrated woman of God. I am a breathing "neon sign" that says, "Hey! God exists! God loves you!" I never thought that my journey would be like this, that I would be called to full-time ministry. That path was for someone who "had their life together," who didn't have my insecurities, my personality quirks, or my interests. I love so-called normal things, like hiking, singing, dancing, baking, writing, watching movies, cooking, playing with animals, working with people, and traveling. So where would a life committed to God "fit" in?

As I have come to discover, my call to religious life has been a string of encounters with God that have helped me see His presence in my life. These encounters have spoken to me of a great and amazing reality: I am loved just as I am. I am called to love God and others just as I am, little ol' me. My coming to embrace and understand this encounter with God's unconditional love and acceptance has felt like I was hitting the jackpot every day. It is a personal love that never fails me, as I have an ever-present Shepherd who guides me through every detail of my life with care; I have a Faithful Friend who accompanies and strengthens me through life's storms. My life is the pursuit of something greater than just me.

I would love to take you with me on a journey of my life. I hope that it will speak in some way to yours. I hope that it will lead you to that awesome realization that, in the final analysis, God is not far away at all. He always has been not far, and in fact, He has always been near you, and will continue to be always. I hope that this allows you to reflect on your life and remember that your life is sacred, you are special, and you have a purpose. I hope that it will also nudge you to embrace with confidence all the experiences of your life, gifts, challenges, and opportunities as worthy platforms to proclaim Christ. Sometimes in our media-driven world—especially in social media—we are tempted to conceal who we truly are because we think we should be someone else or we are not acceptable or simply not "good enough." Christ calls us to be authentically who we are no matter the circumstances, online or offline. By sharing my story, my prayer is that you will see that your life—just as you are—is indeed good enough to be Christ's witness in our world today.

In the Beginning: The Wonders of Childhood

You formed my inmost being; you knit me in my mother's womb. I praise you, because I am wonderfully made; wonderful are your works! My very self you know.

—Psalm 139:13-14

It was about 6:00 p.m. on Sunday in late March when a little girl was born to Raphael and Esther Gitonga at the Aga Khan Hospital in Nairobi, Kenya. My parents had been married five years by then and so my coming joyously broke their long wait for a child. I was born prematurely and had to be placed in an incubator for about two weeks. My mother worried about how small I was and whether I would survive, although her doctor assured her that I would. In fact, even much later, one of our good neighbors at our apartment complex in Nairobi jokingly reminded her of her worries back then with soothing words like, "See, it all worked out!" In accordance with the Kikuyu tribal tradition, as the firstborn girl I was named after my paternal grandmother: *Wairimu.* About a month after I was born, I was baptized Lizzie Jacqueline.

My parents are people of great faith. My dad and his family

are Catholic, while my mom was raised in the Anglican faith and converted to Catholicism when she married. My dear parents had every intention to raise their family in the faith, although I didn't cooperate with that as a toddler. My mother spent most of her Sunday Masses outside the church with me.

I was a little over two years old when my brother was born. As the Kikuyu tribal tradition goes, as the firstborn male in the family, my brother was named after my dad's father: *Wang'ombe*. He was baptized Kevin. Because we were close in age, Kevin and I were "partners in crime" in a lot of mischief growing up. We were little rascals who caused nuisances and thrived on small acts of naughtiness, like cutting up Mom's lipstick or messing up the bathroom. To this day, our apartment in Nairobi bears proof of our childhood curiosities with small locks at the very top of the doors to the bathroom and toilets, clearly marking the sites of long-ago misadventures.

My brother and I had a peaceful childhood, growing up in our farm village home in Nyeri (the central part of Kenya), close to many members of our extended family. We played outside a lot with many of our paternal cousins and often visited our paternal grandparents. All four of my grandparents were an important part of my upbringing, and my parents fostered this connection through visits with my grandparents all through our growing up. Grandpa John, who had been a teacher and school principal, often bestowed his wisdom on us, while Grandma Agnes frequently cooked. She made our traditional tribal dish of beans and corn, as well as roasted corn or sweet potatoes from the three-stone fire in the outside kitchen. Similarly, my maternal grandparents were a delight. Grandpa Hesbon was a retired train driver who reservedly shared his love for life, family . . . and cookies! Grandma Millicent, ever joyful of spirit, never missed a moment to move us to a hearty song, laugh, or dance. At these glorious visits, my brother and I peppered our grandparents with questions and they constantly provided us with fresh insights into our world. It was a treasure to listen to their stories and words of wisdom, while they listened to us as we told our childhood tales. They asked questions, prayed with us, and assured us of their prayers. I am glad my parents insisted on these visits with my grandparents, as they taught me the value of being with my elders, who have so much to share with us and form us if we take time.

Our mother made sure that we also got our fair dose of important life lessons. When not outside playing or visiting family, Kevin and I would watch cartoons after school on our family's small black-and-white television, which drew its power from our car battery, since we did not yet have power in the village. Occasionally we would get so engrossed in these toons that we zapped all the power from the car battery. Our mom would be angry with us the next morning because the car was dead and we would obviously be late to school. Certainly, an important reminder for us to think about how our actions impacted others instead of getting so wrapped in ourselves! I remember another occasion when Mom gave Kevin and me money to go to the nearby shop to buy bread. We set off on our mission, playing along the luscious green grass path amid the flourishing bushes planted on each side, not really paying much attention to what we were doing. Lo and behold, when we arrived at the little shop, we could not find the money! We went back home and my mom would have none of it. She sent us back along the path to find the cash we had lost. While my mom knew it was an impossible mission, it taught us another vital life lesson: *be careful and responsible*. Money did not grow on trees.

When I was eight years old, our family was blessed with a new member, my little sister. As our Kikuyu tribal tradition goes, as the second girl-child in the family, my sister was named after my maternal grandma: *Wanjiru*. She was baptized Susan. With her arrival, it was time for Kevin and me to grow up a little, and we willingly helped take care of Susan (at least we tried—I'm not sure how much "help" we really were). The "call to duty" ranged anywhere from diaper changes to preparing some mashed food or getting some gripe water when Susan had hiccups. Watching and helping my little sister as she grew up was a joy. I still remember how ecstatic Kevin and I were when she learned how to walk, surprising us one day on the path between the cowshed and the house. We could not contain our joy, belting out loud: "She walked! She walked!" We wholeheartedly celebrated this extraordinary thing that happened on such an ordinary day. It's these little life things that added spice and joy to our family life. Throughout my childhood, in the midst of whatever childhood joys or challenges, I always felt very loved by my parents, who gave us the best of who they were to help my siblings and me become who we are today. It was a blessed way to grow up.

The Reality of Life Checks In

My dad was an electrical and communications engineer who worked in Nairobi and used to travel a lot for his job. He eventually started his own residential and small-business alarm-system company. I started school at Mount Kenya Academy (MKA) in Nyeri, attending it for kindergarten through fourth grade. Before Susan was born, my mom, Kevin, and I lived on the farm and would commute daily. At the time, my mom worked as a secretary for the Coca-Cola Company. Kevin and I enjoyed playing near the employee parking lot after school as we waited for Mom to finish work. Every so often we were treated to a tour of the factory. It was fascinating for us to watch the assembly line: the empty soda bottles were crated up and brought into the factory room, where a machine picked up the bottles, which were then washed, assembled in a line, filled, capped, and packed, at which point they were ready for distribution. The best part of our tour was when we got a free soda "fresh off the press," and could drink to our heart's content.

Mom's skills certainly went beyond the secretarial profession. She was a homemaker and an entrepreneur who ran various small businesses and farm projects. Farm projects ranged from growing coffee, corn, beans, vegetables, and fruits to raising chickens, pigs, goats, and cows. She loved to garden, so we had lots of flowers in the homestead and an orchard where we would get different types of fruit. Growing up, Kevin and I did our best to help around the house with different chores, like feeding the cats and dogs. Our dogs were our faithful companions and guarded our home well against strangers. They knew that they could not enter the kitchen, so they often waited patiently outside the kitchen door with hopeful eyes to catch a bite of any great food that might be tossed at them from the kitchen stove. Our cats waited with the dogs, purring as they, too, were eager for treats. The cats on the farm loved milk. It was not unusual to have them meow after you when the cows were getting milked or trail you anxiously as the pail of fresh milk was being brought back into the house. They knew it was breakfast time.

Dad came to our village home on the weekends, so Friday evenings were nights of much anticipation. My brother and I cherished our weekends with Dad. He frequently brought us sweets, like cream wafer cookies from Nairobi or dates and succulent oranges from a trip to Israel. On Sunday morning we attended Mass in our tribal language of Kikuyu at Our Lady of Consolata Cathedral in Nyeri town. It was there that I started my catechism classes. After church, we often stopped at the market to get some tobacco, sugar, bread, and tea leaves before we paid my great-grandma Anastasia a visit; each of us carried one of the items we bought to give her as we entered her little grass-thatched hut.

Grade school years brought opportunities to grow academically and personally. These years were also my first exposure to life's challenges. In my first years at Mount Kenya Academy, I learned French and played the piano. I participated in school assemblies, music competitions, hikes, movies, and art classes. It was a great school to meet students and staff from different ethnic and cultural backgrounds. The student body was diverse and came from other African countries, the United States, Europe, the Middle East, and Asia. My best friend there was an American who had lived in Kenya most of her life. When I was in the fourth grade, my family moved to Nairobi and so I changed schools. We now lived in an apartment, where I was beginning to learn about life in the big city and figuring out the delicate balance of home, school, and social life. Dad challenged us to be disciplined in study and self-improvement, so I attended tutoring sessions to improve my school performance. Neighborhood activities such as dancing and running competitions, riding bikes, or playing rounders (a form of baseball) were a great addition to keeping my growing body active. My parents made sure that I continued with my catechism classes, including my First Reconciliation and my First Holy Communion at the Holy Family Basilica in Nairobi. Throughout my youth, my dad inspired me to grow in my relationship with God through his faithfulness to personal prayer. He was an early riser, faithful to reading the Word of God, praying the rosary before dawn, and then later going to morning Mass daily. He had an active relationship with God and so encouraged my siblings and me to learn how to pray spontaneously to God in our own words. Mom got each of us a Bible and prayer book to aid in this process. Now that my family was in the city, she also enrolled me in Faida, a club for young girls run by Opus Dei women, which provided formation in the Catholic faith, personality development, study, and participation in fun activities such as baking classes and road trips to see national treasures.

Even with these great opportunities for development, I faced many of the same challenges that so many children do, and it was only through God's providence that I was able to make it through. I experienced bullying for the first time at my new school in the city. Things were different and it was difficult to find new friends among the cliques of girls that already existed. The impact of the transition was reflected in my grades. I was not doing well. So my parents decided to take me back to my former school, where, as a boarding student, I continued through eighth grade. The transition back was exactly what I needed to thrive. I was again exposed to great literature, poetry, music, Sunday school, Bible study, and sports. On the weekends, I had time to unwind, going for nature walks or watching TV. I made great friends and enjoyed the familial school environment. Boarding school allowed me a new level of growth in terms of character formation, responsibility, time management, and fostering independence and discipline. I had more time to focus on school and mature as a person.

At the end of eighth grade, I took the Kenya Certificate of Primary Education (KCPE), a national exam. My grades would determine the type of high school I would attend: national, provincial, or local, all of which came with varying opportunities for growth and advancement. I had my eyes set on one of the top national high schools, which had a reputation for outstanding performance.

In the middle of the selection process, I was surprised to receive a visit from the principal, who advised me to choose Kenya High School. I decided to take her advice and I am glad I did. Kenya High School would end up being the perfect fit for what God had in store for my life.

High School Years:
The Search for Truth

Kenya High School became a training ground for the rest of my life in many ways. It was an incredibly rich experience. It was an all-girls national high school, where I met students from all over the country. As is the norm in most Kenyan schools, we wore uniforms: gray skirts and sweaters, brown shoes, white blouses, and red-and-black ties. Our school motto was *Servire est regnare* ("to serve is to reign"), and little did I know that this motto would be realized throughout different moments in my high school years. I was elected to serve my fellow house members as games captain and eventually was elected head of Chania House, my assigned dormitory, as well as serving as ranking member of several other organizations. I also remained active in needlework, French, President's Award hiking, aviation, and typewriting clubs. Continuing my love of physical activity, I plunged into sports such as basketball and I played for the school team throughout high school. I learned a lot from being part of a team, pushing myself hard and engaging in intense workouts, and was able to grow from it, learning valuable life skills in the process. My first time out of the country was a basketball tournament in Zimbabwe. It was an eye-opening experience to see what life looks like in other countries, the different foods, infrastructure, and cultural traditions. As much as I loved sports, the greatest challenge of being an active basketball player was balancing athletics with my studies, responsibilities at school, and my spiritual life.

But my high school years were not all idyllic. I had a crisis of faith during my freshman year, one that would change my relationship with God forever. A few of us first-year girls joined a Bible study with some of the older girls in my house. As the semester went along, I began to question the different aspects of my Catholic faith. *Do Catholics worship Mary? Were all Catholics really going to hell? What kind of God would do such a thing?* I could not reconcile the faith I was learning with the faith I had lived growing up. I felt that my faith was hanging by a thread and so by the end of the second semester, in typical teenage fashion, I decided that I was done being Catholic. During my school holidays, I decided to join another denomination. I went to one of the other church services and felt resolved that I was doing the right thing. Quite confident about the step I had made, I went back home to inform my parents about my newfound faith. When I broke the news to them, they sat me down and told me precious words that have echoed in my life to this day: "You don't need to change your faith, you just need to go deeper."

I went back to school with a turbulent, questioning heart and a deep yearning for clarity. I made an honest prayer from the depths of my being, begging God to please show me the way in the midst of my confusion. And He did in the form of Jesuit seminarians who began teaching my classmates and me during our weekly Confirmation classes. Their instruction was just what I needed. I began to learn more about my faith and became more confident in whom and in what I believed. I wholeheartedly received the Sacrament of Confirmation and took the name Agatha, inspired by the life of the young saint who lived and died a martyr for her faith.

In the same vein, I received great spiritual guidance at the Faida club. This support enabled me to remain faithful in my relationship with God while allowing Him to show me how to develop and use the talents and opportunities that came my way. The rest of my high school years were characterized by growth in my relationship with God in the midst of rigorous classes, basketball tournaments, and leadership responsibilities.

Trying to Find Myself: A Journey from College to Religious Life

Sometimes, where you end up in life doesn't really make sense until you have gone through certain experiences and certain encounters, and you can connect the dots. As I reflect on my journey now, it's clear that certain people and events played an important role as I tried to find myself and figure out God's chosen path for me. These persons have intimately shaped how I view my faith, relationships, identity, and commitment. In fact, these four elements have been the bedrock for me as I authentically strive to be Christ's disciple in person and in social media contexts.

Faith

The kingdom of heaven is like a treasure buried in a field, which a person finds and hides again, and out of joy goes and sells all that he has and buys that field. Again, the kingdom of heaven is like a merchant searching for fine pearls. When he finds a pearl of great price, he goes and sells all that he has and buys it.

—Matthew 13:44–46

It should come as no surprise, my faith in God has been the lens through which I have been able to find meaning and purpose for my life. Simply put, I meet Jesus in different circumstances throughout my day, concretizing the experience of my faith. I find this to be especially vital to me during some of the darker times, when I find that God is closest to me in my struggles. I had one particularly poignant inner battle during the months before I started college. In order to keep busy, I enrolled in a secretarial course to learn basic office and computer skills that would be invaluable for my soon-to-come campus life. While I was flourishing academically, I felt like I had hit a plateau in my spiritual life. One afternoon during one of those difficult prayer moments, I cracked open my Bible and read: "I turned away angry for only a moment, but I will show you my love forever. So says the Lord who saves you" (Isaiah 54:8). I did not quite understand what that meant, but I felt encouraged and relieved through reading it. What would happen oh so subtly after that would change my life forever. Like Saint Paul, I would come to describe this as my "road to Damascus" experience.

Right before I started college, I was invited by "Auntie Ruth," a member of my parish community, to attend a retreat, which provided me with a much-needed spiritual spring cleaning. Rejuvenated, I came out of that experience anew: Mass came alive, the Scriptures brought new meaning into my life, and I learned how to have even deeper conversations with Jesus in Eucharistic Adoration. I felt fortified interiorly to begin my studies in business at Catholic University of Eastern Africa (CUEA).

I remember my college years as a stark depiction of this quest to find everything in a deeper way. As usual, I was active and involved in a plethora of activities in school and church. I had joined the university basketball team—the Penguins—and so hard-core training sessions on weekdays and basketball tournaments on the weekends were the norm. I participated in the Catholic Charismatic Renewal (CCR) prayer group in my parish, served in the core prayer group leadership, engaged in mission work, healing Masses, Gospel crusades, and conferences, and also led the praise and worship ministry. I studied business, with the goal to help others achieve their greatest potential in the workplace.

In the spring of my junior year, I participated in a continuing education retreat for leaders in the CCR in Nairobi. During this retreat, two of the leaders were introduced as "consecrated singles," a phrase that I was unfamiliar with. It sounded appealing, as those persons seemed to belong to God and serve Him wholeheartedly. I was intrigued. Luckily, I was able to learn more at the International Catholic Charismatic Renewal Services (ICCRS) conference in Rome later that year. I felt that the "consecrated single" lifestyle was what I might be called to pursue. I did not quite know what to do with this desire, but it seemed like God had planted a seed there for me, marking it as something to think about as I continued to saunter through life.

Two years later, I graduated college and landed my first job as a health insurance sales consultant. It was a stepping-stone, but was tougher than I had anticipated. I was being paid by commission only and selling health insurance given the Kenyan economy at the time was not easy. The concept of setting money aside for a "rainy day" did not fly for many Kenyans, since many often did not have that much money to spare. I often got discouraged as I struggled to find meaning and purpose for my life. My faith was crucial at this time, reminding me to *hold on. Something better is coming.* I thirsted to give myself to something more integrative: a coherence in my being between what I believed and what I practiced in my work.

I continued to search for meaning, which meant taking a leap into God's loving arms, and looking toward pursuing a master's degree. My mother's cousin had studied at the University of Illinois at Urbana-Champaign, and through his connections there, I came to learn about and submit my application to the Human Resource Education department. It was not long after that that I was accepted into the master of education program. The thought of studying abroad was exciting but also daunting. I had never really lived that far from home. I loved to travel and had even entertained the idea (and made a prayer) to be a missionary. I made up my mind: I would need to take a leap into God's Good Hands.

Identity

Be who God meant you to be and you will set the world on fire.
—*Saint Catherine of Siena*

The journey toward finding my path and my identity really took shape during graduate school. I enjoyed the courses and making friends with people from different parts of the world. I felt like I had landed my dream opportunity and studying Human Resource Development would set me on the right path. I was excited.

Because I didn't know much about US culture before heading to graduate school, one of my greatest fears was whether I would find a Catholic church in which my faith would continue to be nurtured. But of course, God had it all planned out, and I was lucky enough to find Saint John's Catholic Chapel and the Newman Center (often known as Catholic Disneyland) at the university. It truly was a Catholic wonderland because of all the spiritual opportunities that the campus ministry had to offer. There were several Masses a day, opportunities for Eucharistic Adoration and the Sacrament of Reconciliation, retreats, mission trips, spiritual direction, and much more. One of the activities that I participated in was an eight-month discernment retreat aimed at helping participants keep an attentive ear to what God desired of their lives. This intensive retreat consisted of monthly spiritual direction and meetings for prayer, Eucharistic Adoration, teachings on the Catholic faith, and discussions about different life vocations. A talk I attended on religious life and vocations in the church further instilled my desire to explore the "consecrated single" seed that had been planted in my heart. As I continued to discover more and grow in my faith, I decided to continue my studies in Human Resources in a doctoral program. Those extra years helped me grow in self-knowledge. They provided me not only with a firm career path, but also with the fertile ground on which to explore the idea of religious life further.

While I was intrigued by the idea of being a religious sister, I was wary, and talked to God quite honestly about my apprehensions. I did not think I fit the criteria. *God, I think you are kind of late. Don't you call people to this kind of life when they're little? I'm old! Where am I going to find a religious community in this new country? I don't know anyone! Where do I begin?* Well, to God, these objections on my end, while seemingly valid, were really not a problem, and He worked in His own way to make things clearer for me.

The desire to be a religious sister was further refined after I attended a series of career development workshops. As I listened to the presentations and heard about the realities that employees live with and face in different sectors, I could see where my heart more easily aligned itself. I knew that I wanted to be out in the field working with people, helping them to achieve their greatest potential.

My call specifically to the Daughters of St. Paul would crystallize for me during some quite ordinary experiences on campus. For about two years in my doctoral studies, I participated in different "nun runs," which would give me an idea of what religious life entailed. These were weekend visits to different religious communities with a group of young women who were also interested in learning more about religious life. Through the nun runs, I was exposed to different spiritualities, missionary activities, and community types. I was drawn to some and definitely shied away from others. In these interior movements of my heart, it was becoming clearer who I was, and I needed to be faithful to that. Just like when you are dating and looking for a life partner and you often have your list of things that you are looking for in this person, I, too, had my list of things that I was looking for (at least that were musts) in a religious community. You have to ask yourself, *Who are they? What do they do? How do they pray? Why am I attracted to them?* Among my primary criteria were (a) a strong devotion to Eucharistic Adoration; (b) working with and journeying with people on a one-on-one basis to help them reach their potential; and (c) multinational congregation, which allowed ministry in different countries, with different cultures and peoples. I did not know if there was a community out there that would fit all of my criteria, but I was willing to take the time to try to find one.

I had another moment of clarification one day during an unlikely encounter. I got chatting one evening with a mother superior from a Franciscan congregation in Tanzania after the celebration of the twenty-fifth anniversary of priesthood of one of our campus chaplains. I shared with her my journey of discernment, and the sheer number of options that were presented to me. She asked if I had heard of the Daughters of St. Paul, and because I hadn't, I decided to do some research about this community, and eventually contacted the Daughters of St. Paul motherhouse in Boston, who invited me to connect with their Chicago convent, which was the one closest to my campus.

By the end of my visit, I was mesmerized. I felt almost ridiculously peaceful, like I was "among family." I knew that I needed to follow up on what this peacefulness meant. After further correspondence and visits with the sisters, I was introduced to the sister in charge of the Human Resources Department of our Pauline Books and Media Publishing House. We quickly got chatting about human resources and later in our conversations, she invited me to participate in an internship experience. I took the offer for that summer, which became a double blessing for me. I grew in my working-world experience and was able to deepen my knowledge and experience of prayer, community, and ministry of the Daughters of St. Paul by spending time with the sisters.

The biggest clincher of this discernment journey took place after I attended a campus-wide ethics training, where it dawned on me that often there is a discrepancy between knowing what is right and actually doing it. This thought crystallized my understanding of the mission and spirituality of the Daughters of St. Paul. It made sense. The sisters introduce or bring people to a deeper encounter with Jesus Christ, who, once we truly know Him, will help us to be that good parent, honest worker, or diligent religious. Making that connection, I understood that the mission hit at the core of the desire I had to help people reach their fullest potential. Jackpot! I came to the conclusion right then: this is where I wanted to dedicate the rest of my life.

Relationships

But now, thus says the LORD, who created you, Jacob, and formed you, Israel: Do not fear, for I have redeemed you; I have called you by name: you are mine. When you pass through waters, I will be with you; through rivers, you shall not be swept away. When you walk through fire, you shall not be burned, nor will flames consume you.

—Isaiah 43:1-2

Despite how enthusiastic I was about joining the Daughters of St. Paul, there was a thought that nagged at me: *How would I explain this to my family? Would they understand what was going on within me? I* remember breaking the news to my parents—it was met with mixed results. With great caution, my dad's advice would remain constant as he encouraged me to finish my doctoral studies. "Be careful that this is not simply a euphoria." It was even more difficult for my mom. As any mother does, she had her plans as to what I could do with my doctoral degree. Joining religious life would not be anywhere near those dreams. I also felt like I was leaving my siblings in a bit of a lurch. Ours was a community-based culture where family is close; now it seemed like I had abandoned that ship and left the responsibility to my brother and sister. *Who was going to take care of Mom and Dad? How would we handle financial concerns as a family?* It must have felt like they were losing a sister. What kind of God would ask for such a sacrifice? It was painful to watch each of my family members grapple with this next move. I did not understand it fully either, but I knew that it was where God was calling me.

There were also varied reactions from my professors and friends. To some, I was giving my life to a noble cause. It was inspiring. To others, I had pretty much just wasted my entire life. What a waste throwing away all that education, beauty, talent, financial opportunity, and my career to become closed up in a convent! It was hard to hear those things, but I remained steadfast. The call to religious life comes from God and belongs to God, and so He invariably works every detail out for good. I just had to stay put and trust that I was not dreaming all this up. I was banking on Him showing Himself, for real—He would take care of me and my family and friends as well.

Luckily, I had my sisters to help me through this uncertainty and help me stay faithful. In making our religious vows, we commit ourselves to living "in communion" with each of our sisters. This essentially means that although I may not always get along with every single sister in my community, I am always called, by virtue of my spousal relationship with Christ, to love my sister as myself and to seek out her good. Admittedly, that is not always easy, especially where personality or ideological conflicts exist. But those differences could emerge in any situation, and the monthly meetings and visits with the sisters began to deepen my desire to be with them. There was something within me that felt like I was "settling down." I had visited several other communities, but something had drawn me to this one. I even remember one of the vocation directors telling me, "Stay here. Stay with us," which I took as an invitation to go deeper and unearth the vivid attraction I felt to the life and mission of the Daughters of St. Paul. I knew that my heart had found a home in Christ, in the Daughters, who are now my sisters for life.

This call to "stay" reverberates even now at different moments of my religious life, which like any life, has its joys and challenges. Sometimes the challenges can come in the form of disappointments or tensions between what I want and what is being asked of me. Other times they come in the form of family crises or personal upheaval. But it is in these dark moments that I have felt God prop me up through my sisters. This bond we share as brides of Christ reminds me of God's closeness at every moment of life, encourages me to bring a greater attentiveness to my relationships both in and

Sister Amanda Marie Detry, FSP.

Photo courtesy of The Daughters of Saint Paul

Sr. Amanda peeling apples with her fellow Sisters.

Photo courtesy of Sr. Mary Domenica Vitello, FSP.

Sr. Tracey Dugas, FSP (above).
Sr. Tracey's lettering (below).
Photos courtesy of Sr. Tracey Dugas

Sr. Danielle Lussier's first profession.

Sr. Danielle and her parents.
Photos courtesy of Jake Belcher

Sr. Jackie Gitonga, FSP.

Photo courtesy of The Daughters of Saint Paul

Sr. Jackie has some fun.

Photo courtesy of Sr. Jackie Gitonga

Sr. Emily Beata Marsh, FSP.

Photo courtesy of The Daughters of Saint Paul

Sr. Emily embraces being a #MediaNun.

Photo courtesy of Sr. Emily Beata Marsh

Sr. Andrew Taylor with her parents at her first profession (above).
Sr. Andrew at a book exhibition in Italy (below).

Photos courtesy of Sr. Andrew Taylor

Sr. Maria Kim-Ngân Bùi, FSP.
Photo courtesy of The Daughters of Saint Paul

Sr. Maria Kim at her first profession.
Photo courtesy of Sr. Maria Kim-Ngân Bùi, FSP

Sister Julie Marie Benedicta Tuner, FSP.

Photo courtesy of The Daughters of Saint Paul

Sr. Julie and some fellow Daughters of Saint Paul
at their first profession.

Photo courtesy of Sr. Julie Benedicta Turner

outside the community, and prompts me to be authentic in my relationships, both online and offline. That desire to connect does not stop just because I am a religious sister. In fact, it takes on new meaning. All my relationships are in view of Christ and in Christ. Relationships are the place where I meet Christ; they are the concrete corner where God speaks to me. They are also the place where I share Christ's love with others.

Commitment

At the evening of life, we shall be judged on our love.

—Saint John of the Cross

One of the defining moments of my religious life occurred when one of my sisters and I had gone out on mission to bring our books and media resources to a chaplain's conference in the Chicago area. I remember attending the closing Mass, where the key celebrant was the bishop of nearby Gary, Indiana. He shared with us the moving story of how he had had the privilege of taking care of his mother before she died. On her deathbed, his mother looked at his father and asked: "Did I love you enough?" This phrase has stuck with me since then, as it's a reminder that love needs to be at the heart of all I do. It is not the love of material things that gives me happiness and fulfillment in life, but rather the giving of my life to others in love. This is vital to me, as love is at the heart of why I first became a religious sister and why I want to remain a religious sister until my final breath. I have felt the unconditional love and mercy of God on countless occasions. God has not called me to belong to Him in a life of consecration because I am perfect; He has called me because He has loved me. And coming to that knowledge has compelled me to be committed to love before all in every aspect of my life.

When I made my final vows, I went home to my village cathedral, where I began my catechism classes what feels like ages ago. Returning, I could not believe I was being consecrated forever to God in the very church where I could barely reach the holy water font as a little child. It felt like everything had come full circle—God *was* serious about calling me to religious life!

I am all in now and I do not want to turn back. I think I have found what my heart had been looking for and have discovered the greatest Love of an amazing God who has called me to Himself as His bride and disciple forever, just as I am. Through my calling as a Daughter of St. Paul, I have found the place where I can bear witness to Christ more personally, especially using the media through the telling of stories, experiences, challenges, relationships, and new learning moments that have colored different stages of my life path. As a Daughter of St. Paul, I feel constantly drawn out of myself to creatively give of myself to God and others in love. I am filled with gratitude and amazement at a simple glance at parts of my life story because God is so tangible. My prayer is that you will discover the same.

My Love Is Your Life, Child

My Child:
When you awake, My Love awakens you
    and breathes new life
That your designs may be fruits of love
That your words may be words of love
That your acts may be acts of love

When you pray, My Love prays in you
To commune with me with a heart of love
To make your self-offering out of love
To repent for offenses against love

When you reach out, My Love reaches out
    through you
That they may feel My Love in your love
That they may see My Love in your love
That they may hear My Love in your love

And when you rest, My Love rests in you
To heal your love and make it whole
To restore you to new life
To keep you secure

And when you finally lay to rest
You will fall back into My arms of Love
From whence you came
And where you will be forever and ever

LIFE IS *a* GIFT *from* GOD—
HOW WILL YOU USE IT?

SR. EMILY BEATA MARSH, FSP

*S*o, *I think God is calling me to be a sister . . . but how do I know for sure?*

This is the question that circled through my mind and heart over and over when I was eighteen years old. It's the question that, with a bit of fear and trembling, I asked the vocation director of the Daughters of Saint Paul. I had been visiting the sisters on and off for about a year, and I felt God calling me to do more. Years later, I now serve as the vocation director for the Daughters, speaking about vocations, organizing discernment retreats, and meeting regularly with women who are discerning religious life more seriously; it's the question that I hear from almost all the young women who talk to me about religious life. It's a question that I understand intimately, having undergone my own journey to find the answer for my life. But to get from there to here, we have to go back a little way.

I grew up in a small town outside of Buffalo, New York. (And when I say "small," I really mean small. It is the type of place that boasts a single, flashing traffic light, where the post office, church, library, and grocery store are all located within a block of each other, where my dad owns the local grocery store and the town mayor is also the dishwasher repairman, and essentially everyone knows everyone else. You get the picture.)

Although my hometown is tiny, my family is quite big—I'm the oldest of twelve children. Yes, you read that right: twelve, as in a dozen, or double the size of the Brady Bunch. So it should come as no surprise that family life was a really important part of my upbringing. I loved having so many brothers and sisters. When I was little, I always had playmates, and as I got older, I loved that I had so many people who understood me and who really knew me.

Growing up, my siblings and I all worked part-time at my dad's store, stocking shelves, running the register, and scooping ice cream at the ice cream window. At any given moment on a summer evening, there could be (and still are today!) two or three or four Marsh kids working together. When we weren't working, or doing schoolwork, or playing outside, you could often find us Marshes at the local parish church. Every Sunday at the 11 a.m. Mass, you could find us in the first pew on the right-hand side (which gradually became the first two pews as the family kept growing). When

I was eleven years old, I graduated to the organ bench and became the parish organist for that Mass.

Outside of Mass, my family was quite involved in our parish and our faith was an important part of our daily lives. My father served year after year as a contact person for various parish outreaches and helped grill the hamburgers and hot dogs for the annual parish picnic. My mom taught my siblings and me that God wasn't just for Sundays—once or twice a week, on a random Tuesday or Friday, she would pack us all up and take us to Mass—and also showed us how to pray every evening before bed. My brothers were altar servers and my sisters sang in the choir. When I reached high school, I helped to teach religious education, and as soon as I could drive, I started attending daily Mass before school.

Outside of church, I got into music at a fairly young age, taking piano lessons at eight years old. Playing piano was, and continues to be, one of my favorite activities. I continued lessons through high school, majored in music for two years in college before I entered the convent, and now in the convent, I often play piano or organ for all our big feast days and celebrations.

I also played soccer for many years and was a member of a rec team every summer from the time I was about ten years old until I graduated high school. While a robust "athletic career" was never in the cards for me, soccer kept me active with other kids my age, and rounded out my already busy life. All in all, I lived a pretty normal small-town life.

Throughout my formative years, weaving through my busy

life, thoughts about my future started to take shape. I'm a Type A planner—I'm similar to my mom in that regard. I've always liked to make lists and schedules and plans and contingency plans and backup contingency plans for every facet of my life. So naturally, when it came to my future, I thought that I had things figured out well in advance. I was going to finish high school, go to college, major in English, and probably become an English teacher, ideally at a Catholic high school in some idyllic imaginary town not far from where my parents lived. That was the plan, at least. To riff on a phrase from an old Jewish saying, make plans and God laughs.

What Does God Want Me to Do?

This was the first—of many—question that entered my mind when I started thinking and rethinking about my future. Actually, I should say that this question entered my heart wordlessly long before it entered my mind. As I went about my life, I had a sense that I was meant to live for more than just myself and my plans. This certainly included living for others, and meant giving back in some way, a value that my parents instilled in my siblings and me from an early age. In some way, it also included living for God.

Sitting here and typing this, many years (and many hours of reflection) after the fact, I am able to recognize this yearning more clearly. In the moment, however, all I had was just a vague sense that my life was meant to be about more than just me. Gradually, that vague sense coalesced into a question. I began to ask, *What does God want me to do?*

That was a scary question. It seemed to open up a great big void in front of me. I knew what I wanted to do. But if I asked God what he wanted me to do . . . how would I know what he wanted? And even if I figured out what he wanted . . . what if it wasn't what *I* wanted?

Today, in some ways, I sit on the other side of that question. I say "in some ways" because the question of what God wants me to do is one that is with me every day. On one hand, the "big" answer is taken care of—I know that God wants me to be a religious sister with the Daughters of St. Paul. But each day there are smaller answers to that question. Sometimes they are as small as how he wants me to respond to an email or whether he wants me to sign up to cook supper tonight. Other times it's bigger things, like whether to say yes to a new role or assignment, or even be transferred overseas. In every decision, I bring God into the equation, asking him each step of the way, each minute of the day, what is it that you want me to do? How should I approach this, God? What should I do next?

In my experience as vocation director and in my conversations with young women discerning the vocation to religious life, these questions are the keys of the journey of discernment. The big question tends to surface first—what does God want me to do? This question leads to other big, scary, gaping questions: How will I know? What if I don't like it? Will I be happy?

The key to coming to the answers is asking the big question in the face of small moments. What I mean by this is that if a young woman feels compelled to ask what God wants her to do, but is overwhelmed by the vastness of this question, then it is helpful to add one small word to the end of the question: What does God want me to do NEXT? My experience has taught me that the answers can be surprising. God might simply want you to spend more time with him. He might want you to be more honest with him. He might inspire you with a particular prayer practice or a concrete way to be of service to others. Often, he simply wants our presence. He can work with that.

In my own life and discernment, I was overwhelmed by the question of what God wanted me to do. But when I reflected on what God wanted me to do *next*, answers came much more readily. They felt like small answers, but they were answers nonetheless. Read Scripture every day. Keep talking to the vocation director. Be present to my family, my schoolwork, my extracurricular activities. And the biggest one: remember often how much God loves me. Sometimes I was frustrated by these answers, because they didn't seem to be getting me anywhere. But I could see that they were helping me to grow closer to God, and over time I saw that they had opened me to listen to God and to hear the "bigger" answer.

I've learned that sometimes we expect big answers when God wants us to start small. We want the answer to what our vocation is, and God wants to give us this answer. But he also wants to take us on the journey of finding this answer, and starting this journey means spending time with him, learning to remain in his presence, and learning to be loved by him.

What Is It Like to Be a Sister?

The question of what God wanted me to do is what initially led me to visit the Daughters of St. Paul. I had first met the sisters when I was in eighth grade, when they gave a vocation talk at a youth conference I was attending. After that conference, I signed up for their mailing list and received a magazine with stories about the sisters. I kept up with them for a few years after that, and when I was sixteen years old, I received an invitation to the St. Paul Summer Program, the Daughters' annual summer discernment program for young women in high school. When I first attended, the program had already been going for a few years, and we still run it today. It's a weeklong program that invites high school women to live with the sisters at the motherhouse in Boston, experience their prayer and mission, and have some fun in the process.

This program answered many questions that I had about discernment, religious life, and the Daughters of St. Paul in general. But perhaps the biggest question it answered was, What is it like to be a sister? What is a typical "day in the life"?

In my work now as vocation director, I have probably answered that question hundreds of times. By phone, by email, at talks, and on social media, young women are always asking, What is it like to be a sister? This is an important question in what I call the "information-gathering phase" of discernment. That is, it is a necessary part of discernment that is simply about learning all the options.

So what are these options? For a Catholic woman striving to understand how God is calling her to love him and love others, and figuring out how to respond to that call, these options are marriage, the single life, or the religious life. Every person is single at some point, so we all know what that is like. We also generally have some idea (whether it is flawed or otherwise) of what marriage is like, or at least what it can be like. But religious life? If you're anything like me, the only things I knew about sisters, until I first met one as a preteen, I had learned from holy cards and biographies of saints. So a young woman who is trying to learn about religious life at some point needs to ask a sister: What is your day like?

There are many ways to ask this question, and even more ways to get it answered. In our Daughters of St. Paul convents, we receive dozens of inquiries each week via email and social media, and many are asking that initial question: What is it like to be a sister? For anyone curious, perusing the websites, social media, and videos of religious communities will give you a great sense. If you're earnest or want to learn more, a good old-fashioned telephone call to the vocation director of the community you're interested in will give you an even better sense. But for any young woman seriously considering this life, nothing will give you hands-on experience of a day in the life of a sister like actually living a day in her life when you visit a community. Most communities have "Come and See" experiences for exactly this purpose.

As a young woman, despite my already robust plans for the future, I increasingly became aware that I needed to investigate the path toward religious life. The St. Paul Summer Program was that kind of experience for me, allowing me access to the day-to-day of religious life. That week other young women and I prayed morning and evening prayer with the sisters, went to Mass with them, ate breakfast, lunch, and supper together (yes, in the convent we do call it supper). We had classes with different sisters, worked in the Daughters of St. Paul publishing house (imagine how happy my nerdy little bookworm heart was when I got to read short-story submissions for our children's magazine!), watched movies, and took walks. And every day, we prayed an Hour of Adoration together. I was living a "day in the life . . ." and I loved it. More than that, I was having the best week of my life. But as the months and years passed after that week, and I reflected on what I had experienced and felt (discernment and general life pro-tip—always reflect on what you've experienced afterward!), I realized that I had learned three significant things that week.

First, the sisters were normal. And friendly. And funny! I felt right at home with them. I wanted to come back and visit with them again. As the vocation director probably told me back then, and as I tell young women now, feeling at home in and of itself is not necessarily a sign that God is calling you to enter that community, but it certainly could be a sign that he wants you to take a closer look at something. So, take that closer look.

Second, I learned how to pray. I know that's a big and somewhat nebulous statement, but I don't say it lightly. That week really taught me how to pray. I already had a foundation from my family life. I knew my prayers, and I knew that I could talk to God. What I didn't know, and what I started to learn that week, was how to listen to God and how to recognize his voice. During that summer program, we prayed an Hour of Eucharistic Adoration every day. (Catholics believe that Jesus is truly and bodily present in the Holy Eucharist, and Eucharistic Adoration is prayer in the presence of Jesus in the Eucharist. The Daughters of St. Paul pray for an hour before the Eucharist every day, which we call our "Visit with Jesus," because it's meant to be a true visit with the most important person in our lives.) Additionally, we also learned about and prayed with the Bible. Both of these practices taught me how to listen. They taught me that God was interested in me and spoke to me. From watching the sisters at prayer, I saw that their prayer was a conversation with someone who loved them and whom they in turn also loved. My prayer wasn't like that yet, but I wanted it to be.

Now, when a young woman talks to me about her discernment, the first piece of advice that I give is to pray, because while prayer is basic and essential at all times in the spiritual life, it becomes even more crucial in a time of vocational discernment. Prayer is the foundation, the context, the content, and the very air of a relationship with God. It is where we learn what God's voice sounds like, and where we learn what we sound like as we express ourselves and our reality to God. The founder of the Daughters of St. Paul, Blessed James Alberione, used to say, "Prayer is the breath of the soul." And the soul needs to breathe!

In relearning to really pray, I realized that prayer is to speak with and listen to God, and there are some things that really helped me to do that. There are some things that can be generally helpful in growing in prayer. First, choose a time to pray. The goal, according to my community's namesake, St. Paul, is of course to "pray always" (1 Thessalonians 5:17), but we need to start somewhere! Have a concrete time that is set aside for prayer. Further, make sure to speak to God in your own words. Tell him what you think, what you're feeling—even (and especially) if you're not feeling that great. Honesty with ourselves, and with God, cannot be overemphasized. Equally important, leave time to listen to God in silence. I know that silence can be uncomfortable. Actually, let's just say it: silence is uncomfortable. But God needs our silence so that he can reveal things to us—things about himself, about ourselves, about what we're praying about. Prayer is a crucial, life-giving conversation with God, and you cannot live a spiritual life without it.

The third thing that I learned during my week at the St. Paul Summer Program was that there was no wrong age to start thinking about what God wanted for me. I asked every sister I met that week, why did you become a sister? And one thing that I noticed was that many of their answers began, "Well, I first started thinking about it when I was young," or, "I first met the sisters when I was fifteen," or, "I entered right after high school . . ." Besides impressing upon me that women my own age could start thinking and praying and making decisions about their life, it also gave me permission to think and pray seriously about my own life. It is never too early, or too late, to ask God, *What do you want for me?*

Okay, I'm Discerning . . . What Should I Do Now?

After my first St. Paul Summer Program, more questions arose. Without a doubt, the biggest and most pressing was: *Now what?* I knew that I had thoroughly enjoyed my week with the sisters. And I knew that I definitely wanted to go back. But what did that mean for my future? Even more, what did it mean for my present? What should I do about it?

In reflecting on these questions now, I've come to understand, through years of asking for and receiving answers to these internal queries, that God is the one who guides me. At the time, though, I was pretty clueless. If you had asked me if I was "discerning," I probably would have said no. I'm honestly not sure that I even knew what that word meant at the time (although I would come to know in the course of my discernment). What I did know was that I had encountered God in a powerful way, and I wanted to keep encountering him. This is how God kept his hand on me and guided me.

The vocation director at the time could see that I had had a powerful experience of God and was committed to growing in my relationship with him. She offered to continue speaking with me on a regular basis. We talked by phone once a month, and as I shared what I was praying about and what I felt, I gradually grew more accustomed to understanding God's voice and to speaking about my spiritual life. It was a process that was filled with much reflection, some growing pains, and ultimately much peace.

This is the process that I guide dozens of young women through in my current role with the Daughters. The question of *Now what?* is one that often follows a "peak" experience. When someone realizes (or accepts) for the first time that God may be calling them to consider religious life, or when they go on a retreat and have a beautiful or clarifying experience, or when they tell someone for the first time, "I think God is calling me to be a sister"—all of these are powerful, life-changing experiences. Then they go back to their daily life as a student or an accountant or a graphic designer (or in my case a junior in high school), and it's not clear how that experience should affect their daily life.

This is something I often talk about with the women who get in touch to talk about their discernment. Often, when a young woman emails, or DMs, or calls, she is asking some version of the *Now what?* question. There is no "one size fits all" answer to this question. However, there are a few things that are helpful to keep in mind when choosing your own life path, especially if you are discerning religious life.

First, last, and always, PRAY. Second, in prayer, follow your encounters with God. I know that's kind of an odd expression, but it's the best way I've found of expressing how to figure out which way to go in vocational discernment. When you find that you are encountering God in a particular way (praying in silence, for example) or in a particular area (reflecting on a certain area of your life), it is helpful to stay with that. Not exclusively, and not stubbornly, but to put it plainly, if God is speaking, listen! Sometimes we feel God whispering something to us, and we are too quick to move on, to think about what we should do next, or how we should put what we hear into practice. There is a time for this, but first, keep listening.

And keep asking the question *Now what?* Ask it of God. Ask it of yourself. Ask it of your friends and family. Then it's a question of what to "do" with the answers. This is often less complicated than we think it is. After I returned from that first St. Paul Summer Program, I began to find ways—little ways—to be of service, especially in my parish. I played the organ and sang in the choir. I volunteered to teach fourth-grade catechism. I even used to stay after Mass on Sundays to help count the collection. I don't really know what possessed me as a sixteen-year-old to enjoy (yes, enjoy!) spending my Sunday afternoons counting change with a bunch of sixty- and seventy-year-old ladies. I do know that I was starting to truly enjoy being around the church and giving of myself and branching out for the sake of others. This is the movement that is important to nurture when you're discerning specifically, or generally looking toward next steps in life. Find ways to go out of yourself. It could be volunteering at your parish, like I did; it could be volunteering at a soup kitchen; it could be as simple as baking cookies for your family or spending time with your parents even though you don't really have the time. The pattern of going out of yourself turns you more toward God, and in that turning, the path becomes clearer and clearer.

Do I Really Want This?

After a year of meeting regularly with the vocation director, and visiting the sisters about every six months, I felt strongly that I was meant to spend my life as a Daughter of St. Paul. But I still had doubts. Even though I felt called, I wasn't sure if the sisters felt that way ... or even if God felt that way, when I really thought about it! This was probably the biggest doubt of my discernment: Was this really something that God wanted for me, or was it just something that I wanted for myself? With this in my mind and heart, I returned to Boston to visit the sisters as a seventeen-year-old senior in high school who half thought that she wanted to ask to apply to the community, and half thought that she was making it all up in her head.

It was a fun, grace-filled week. The sisters took us on a road trip to visit our community in New York City, my first time there. While I enjoyed all the fun we were having, underneath it, I loved being back in the rhythm of religious life, with a daily Hour of Adoration and daily prayer with the Scriptures. I remember feeling like Jesus was right beside me, living that week with me.

On one of the final nights Sister Margaret, the vocation director leading the week, said, "Tomorrow will be our day of silent retreat." I was excited. I had always had powerful experiences of God on my silent retreats with the sisters. And of course, I had a big question on my heart to bring to God in prayer: Was he really calling me? Should I take the next step?

I don't remember everything about that day of silent retreat. But there is one particular moment that I will always remember. The silent retreats that the sisters guided us on were always based on praying with Scripture. We received several prayer guides throughout the day that suggested Scripture passages to pray with. One that I received that day suggested the Gospel of Matthew, chapter 14.

This Gospel passage recounts the story of Jesus walking on water. After a full day, Jesus sends the disciples out onto the sea in the boat while he goes up a mountain to pray. While the disciples are out in the boat, a huge storm comes up. As they're fighting the storm, in the middle of the night, they see a figure walking toward them. Is it Jesus? Peter speaks up. "Lord, if it is you, command me to come to you on the water. [Jesus] said, 'Come'" (Matthew 14:28).

In that moment, I realized . . . I was Peter. I was in my boat, and Jesus was beckoning to me from the water. Just as Peter had asked, I, too, was asking, *Lord, is it you? Are you calling me to give my life to you as a Daughter of St. Paul? Because if you are, I will! But how will I know that you are? Lord, is it you?* And in my prayer, I felt Jesus' answer in my heart—the same answer he had given to Peter: *Come.* Not, *Yes, Emily, I am calling you to be a Daughter of St. Paul.* Not, *Here, Emily, let me show you exactly how your life will unfold.* Just that one simple word: "Come." I felt so much peace at that. Jesus wasn't calling me to be absolutely sure at that moment. He simply wanted me to trust him enough to take the next step without knowing the step after that, trusting that he would continue to guide me and to show me one step at a time.

Inspired by this encounter with Jesus, I went to speak to the vocation director that afternoon. I told her that if she thought the time was right, I wanted to apply to enter the community. After praying about it herself, she agreed that I could begin the application process.

How Do I Hear God's Voice?

This doesn't mean that everything was smooth sailing after that, or that I always felt perfectly at peace, or that I didn't have any more doubts. There were plenty of bumps in the road, plenty of times when I wasn't sure if I should be doing this. When we are making any major decision, obstacles, doubts, and uncertainties are things to pay attention to. They are, believe it or not, one way that God has of communicating with us. Sometimes God uses an obstacle to point us in a different direction. Or he may use our doubt or confusion to show his love and presence for us in a new way.

It's important not to bury our doubts. We need to talk about the obstacles and doubts we are experiencing—first with God, then with someone we trust. Don't be afraid of the doubts. They help us to be real with God, and they are certainly ways that God uses to encounter us and direct us.

My fundamental doubt when I went to visit the sisters that summer was that I still wasn't sure I was hearing God correctly. I was sure about what I wanted: I wanted to become a Daughter of St. Paul. But I was nowhere near sure about what God wanted. This uncertainty propelled another question, one that I asked many times, and one of the most frequently asked questions that I hear as a vocation director: *How do I hear God's voice?*

This is a big question with a multifaceted answer. I would like to start by simply stating that every person can hear God's voice. We are God's creatures, and we have within us the capacity to communicate with him. We can speak with him, and we can hear him when he speaks to us. So the question becomes, *How does God speak to us?*

Think about yourself, and how you communicate. What is unique to you when you speak, or when you listen? I know for myself that I tend to nod a lot when I listen. I try to speak clearly. Just as we communicate in a manner unique to us as individuals, God also communicates in a manner characteristic to him. He speaks through Scripture. He also speaks—and listens—through the events of our lives, so it is helpful to reflect on the daily happenings in your life simply by asking yourself, *How was God present in my day?*

Furthermore, there are also individual, unique ways in which God communicates with each of his creatures. Two examples come to mind for me. In my prayer, God often takes what I am saying to him, and starts saying it to me. The second, which will show you my nerdy side, is that God sometimes speaks to me through grammar! In my prayer with Scripture, sometimes what strikes me are the words or actions of Jesus; sometimes it's the simple placement of a comma, or the tense of a verb. This might not mean much of anything to someone else, but to me it means the world. This is God speaking directly to me.

So while the question *How do I hear God's voice?* can become *How does God speak to us?* the question of how to hear his voice still remains, and there are things that we can do to open ourselves to hearing God's voice. First—and this is no surprise—is prayer. If possible, our prayer should be daily. There is something about committing to a daily practice that reminds us that we are always in relationship with God every day. Think about other relationships in your life. When people are important to us, we make sure that we communicate with them often. It is the same with God—when our relationship with God is important to us, we make sure that we commit to nurturing that relationship regularly.

As I have mentioned before, the regular practice of silence also helps us to hear God's voice. Silence is tricky because at first it seems like we're not doing anything and we can be tempted to give up on it. But silence is fruitful even when it seems like nothing is happening, as eventually our silence opens up a wide enough space for us to hear God's voice more and more clearly. These moments of silence are also good opportunities to examine our day or to take some extra time to reflect when we find that we've had an especially strong experience, either positive or negative. One indication of a strong experience is that it usually leaves us with a strong emotion. Rather than avoiding these emotions, or wallowing in them (the two extremes), we can use them as a signal that there's something we need to reflect on and bring to God. We can ask ourselves, *Why am I feeling this way? What happened recently? How do I feel about it? What would I like to tell God about it? What would I like to hear from God?* I can assure you that God will meet us in our own experiences. This is a powerful way to encounter him because it tells us that he is not afraid of getting involved in our lives.

How Will I Know
What Community to Choose?

After I began the application process for the Daughters of St. Paul, I continued to grow in my relationship with God, in my own self-knowledge, and in my conviction of being called. I also continued to learn about the Daughters of St. Paul's mission, what they did, and how they lived. At this point, the questions that came to me weren't internal; instead, they were coming from the people in my life as they learned that I was applying to enter a religious community.

The most common of these questions that people asked me was some form of: *How (or why) did you choose the Daughters of St. Paul?* This is a question that I still hear today from young women coming to talk to me about religious life. They want to know how and why I chose my community, because they themselves are trying to understand how and why to choose a particular community.

This might sound kind of clichéd, but I have always felt that I didn't choose my community so much as God chose me for it. Don't get me wrong, my free will had something to do with it, too! I freely chose to discern with the Daughters of St. Paul, to ask to apply, and to respond to God's invitation to enter formation and eventually make vows. What I mean is that I know God created me to be a Daughter of St. Paul, and placed people and events and circumstances in my life to help me discover this. God has a vocation, a special call, for each person. Responding to this call gives God the greatest glory, brings us the greatest happiness, and helps us to love and serve others in the best way possible.

In that sense, I came to a point where I realized that I couldn't not be a Daughter of St. Paul if I wanted to fully be the person God created me to be. After visiting time and again with the sisters, I realized that not only could I be myself when I was with the sisters, but also that I would become more and more myself as a sister. This was a vital distinction for me and it is an important point in any journey of discernment, because God does not call us to stay exactly as we are, but to grow and to change and to live every day more in love with him and more united to him.

How Do I Stay Open to What God Wants?

Other questions that come up when a young woman gets a little bit deeper into discernment of religious life and discernment of a particular community often have to do with freedom. Questions such as, *How do I stay open to what God wants? How do I know if God is confirming something, or if I'm just looking too hard for a sign? Should I date/take a new job/move to a new apartment/(insert your own question here) while I'm considering religious life?*

These are questions that I certainly asked during my discernment. So I know that at the core of these questions is often an unexpressed and even unknown desire and need to remain free while choosing to give my freedom to another, in this case God. This can feel like a conflict at times. How can I simultaneously remain free while giving my freedom away? In the Christian view of freedom, we are free not in order to do whatever we want; we are free in order to choose the good. Sometimes that good is to give myself freely and totally over to God.

This concept of freedom is crucial for discernment. We all have certain attachments that limit our freedom. At the beginning of my discernment, I was attached to my own view of my life. We might be attached to our own routines, to wanting to know what comes next, to certain comforts, or to any number of things.

The key is a process of becoming aware of the attachment, reflecting (in prayer but also with the help of another person, for example a spiritual director) on why I am so attached to that, and little by little letting it go. And then I am that much freer to choose what God wants for me.

Life Is a Gift of God—How Will You Use It?

At the end of all the questions, I want to leave you with one piece of advice that I received during my own discernment, and with one final question. The piece of advice is this: there is no question that we need to be afraid of, or that will not eventually be answered, as long as we keep our eyes fixed on Jesus. So dive into the questions, because often that's precisely where Jesus wants to lead us.

The final question is one proposed by Blessed James Alberione: "Life is a gift of God—how do you want to use it?" Without knowing it, I asked myself this question in different ways throughout my discernment. Even now, this is a question that I return to and ask myself every so often. In fact, I have it on the bulletin board in my office where I can see it every day. It gives me clarity and reminds me that God and I are collaborating on my life. My life is a total gift from him, and he wants my total involvement as I strive to give it back to him. This, after all, is vocation—giving my life back to God in love, little by little, day by day, until I belong totally to him.

A HABIT
OF COMING HOME

SR. K. ANDREW MARIE TYLER, FSP

There's this verse in the Gospel of John where Jesus says, "In my Father's house there are many rooms, and I am going to prepare a place for you" (John 14:2). We might not be used to thinking that Bible verses actually have anything to do with our daily lives. But my whole "story" has revolved around these words of Jesus, even when I was completely oblivious to them. Throughout my life, I can see the ways in which my heart has been searching for its true home, and the ways in which Jesus has been leading me there all along. In fact, this isn't something he's done just for me: the Lord prepares a place for each one of us, with all of our gifts and positive traits, as well as all of our faults, all of the things that we'd rather gloss over completely. I hope by the time you finish hearing my story, you'll hear him speak these words to you, too, in the depths of your heart: "I am going to prepare a place for you."

But I'm getting ahead of myself. If I were to ask you what comes to mind when you think about home and family, what would you say? Maybe it is a certain house or apartment. Maybe it is the people who inhabited that place: your parents and grandparents, brothers and sisters, extended family and close friends.

Now let's switch it up a bit. If I were to ask you to imagine the childhood home and family life of a nun, what images come to your mind this time? I mean, where do nuns come from? Do we grow up in a church? Did my family home look like a convent, with austere corridors, light streaming through stained glass windows, my family members gathering regularly for solemn prayer? Okay, maybe you didn't imagine something that extreme. But lots of people don't know what to think when it comes to faith-filled persons. People sometimes assume that I come from a stereotypically big Catholic family where we prayed a lot, and my parents must have talked to me about being a sister from a young age. But like every person in every walk of life, each sister has a unique journey, a unique home and family that have contributed to her story. I didn't grow up in a convent (no one does!), I'm not from a big Catholic family (though I know lots of awesome people who are!), and I didn't even go to church as a kid. Most years my family didn't even go to Mass on Christmas or Easter; I like to joke that we were very consistent in *not* going to church! The Lord had to be pretty creative to lead this Texan drummer with a black belt to find her home with Jesus among the Daughters of Saint Paul. And that's just what he did. This life is where I have found my home in Jesus, and with that came a deeper sense of family than I had ever known. But it wasn't always smooth travel—there was a lot of searching and some detours in order to get to this place, the place that Jesus had prepared for me.

My First Experience of Home

As I reflect on my life, I can see that in many instances my idea of family was a bit flawed. We all know there is no such thing as a perfect family, and I, like I'm sure many of you, have both good and bad memories of my childhood. I always considered myself to have come from a good home, blessed to have had almost everything I could have wanted. I have wonderful memories of playing baseball with my dad (I wanted to be the next Mickey Mantle or Nolan Ryan!) and of listening to fun music with my mom, especially the good stuff like the Beatles or the Beach Boys! Despite this, I was searching for something else, something that would fulfill my deepest longings and desires of my heart. Ultimately, I was searching for something that could not be completely attained by myself alone. I was searching for a family, for a home, for a community, because I hadn't really felt some of those things while growing up. I was raised in Texas as an only child, and when I was ten years old, my parents divorced. At the time, it was a complete surprise to me.

My life seemed to change overnight, and looking back, I see that it would be many years before I truly felt at home. From the time of my parents' divorce, I would always long for a home that was permanent, that would not be suddenly upended by other people's decisions. I longed for a place that was "prepared for me," but I just didn't think it was possible to find this. And not only did I not think it was possible, but the amazing promise of Jesus wasn't anywhere on my radar then.

Suddenly, after the divorce, I had two of everything: two beds, two houses, two backyards, two celebrations of every holiday. Some of this was good; what kid doesn't like two birthdays, with two cakes and twice the number of presents? But there was an element to this existence that made me feel unstable, as neither of these homes ever felt permanent, like they were "mine." Both my parents remarried people of Mexican-American descent. Although I have come to embrace this part of my identity and to deeply appreciate Mexican culture and traditions, it was initially a bit of a culture shock. The first few holidays my mom and I spent with my now-stepfather's family, there was lots of Spanish spoken and I felt a bit unable to engage, like I was always one step behind. It was as if I was an observer standing on the outside looking in and trying to see where I fit in. And the sheer size of my new family was, at times, overwhelming. Gatherings went from the small trio of my mother, my father, and me to occasions with so many cousins and aunts and uncles that I couldn't keep track of everyone.

I smiled through it all, and as a child, I remember being complimented on having handled my parents' divorce so well, but the truth was, I didn't know what to do besides put on a brave face. Although seemingly overnight the number of people in my life had astronomically increased, I felt like I wasn't seen, known, and loved in quite the same way I had been before. So, as I grew up I longed for a place where I belonged, a place where I could be my-self without seeking and without having to feel like I had to prove myself and without having to be always connected to another per-son's approval. Sometimes feeling at home is something as simple as not having to explain that I'm there because I'm so-and-so's wife's kid. I wanted to be known not for who I was related to but for who I was. Without even knowing it, I was about to embark on a quest to find the place "prepared for me" beyond the confines of my family. The trouble is, I didn't know where I was going. As the Apostle Thomas put it to Jesus: "We don't know where you are going; how can we know the way?" (John 14:5).

I didn't know my destination—my home—for the longest time. I went from one thing to the next, trying in vain to find my way. In the Lord's mercy, I eventually got there. But no journey is a straight, direct line. Mine certainly wasn't.

Finding Temporary Homes

Music has always been a part of my life. At a young age, I was able to join the school band, choosing to play the drums. (I'm sure my parents were thrilled.) I liked the drums because they seemed cool, but also, they seemed different from any other instrument I could choose from. They actually involved much more than just playing on one drum. There were cymbals, snare drums, base drums, and eventually the whole drum set. In time I joined my school jazz band on the drum set. I kept with it in the years that followed, and it really became an outlet for me, an activity in which I found joy and pride in doing something well. Part of growing up is finding a place where you feel seen as an individual, and I felt this way playing music. Since I wasn't especially good at the academic side of school, it helped that I was musically talented, as it gave me confidence. It helped me stay positive, as there was something I could do well, a way that I could make something beautiful. I also loved music because it felt like a whole other language through which I could understand and express myself in a way that I hadn't experienced before.

Even further, there was also a special type of closeness that I had with the other band students and we formed a sort of community with deep friendships that lasted for years. Being part of the school band, I was able to do my part and contribute to something that was much bigger than myself, and be noticed for it. I dreamed of taking it further, studying music at Berklee in Boston. For a long time, I thought that that would be my path, that it was my final destination, that it was what was really God's gift to me. Even if I didn't think of God much in my day-to-day life at this point, I figured music was a gift from God to me, and that through it, I would find the way to be completely happy and discover my purpose in life. Because really, everyone wants to be happy and have a purpose, right?

I also felt seen, and found another sort of family, through participating in martial arts. From a young age I had always wanted to practice karate. A true child of the eighties, I was initially inspired by *The Karate Kid* and *Teenage Mutant Ninja Turtles*; I was a proud member of the Ninja Turtles fan club, and as a younger kid, my friends and I would pretend to be them! But over the years the desire to actually learn martial arts never went away. I thought it would be both a challenge and a way to learn how to defend myself. When I was eleven years old, I started karate lessons. The school was a very traditional Okinawan- and Japanese-style karate school and it was a lot of hard work, but I truly loved it! I was able to earn rank as I progressed, eventually attaining the rank of second-degree black belt. It required hours of practice and discipline, but from the moment that I passed I felt like I really belonged somewhere. One example of this came about when I was testing for my first-degree black belt for the second time—I had failed the first test six months previously and had worked so hard to be ready for this second try. Many of my classmates helped me prepare. Finally, at the end of the exam, all of us who tested for different ranks were at attention awaiting the results from our instructor; when he got to me and said I passed, all of a sudden the student behind me got so excited that he picked me up and swung me around in complete happiness. Just in case you were wondering, that kind of thing didn't normally happen, especially during a formal ceremony! In that moment I realized that I had found the family I was searching for. There were many "brothers" (I was one of two girls in the class), who I assumed would be a part of my life from there on out. After we'd spent hours and hours training together, I found that I could be myself in karate school. Even when I would come back to town from college, I would always be welcomed with open arms.

Steps Toward Home

I had attended Catholic school since first grade and so had learned *about* Jesus. But I didn't really *know* him until high school. It was kind of like the way we might know our favorite actors or professional sports players. We can know a lot *about* them—where they live, where they went to school, how old they are, or how many siblings they have. But we don't really *know* them personally, as friends or as people. This is how I thought about Jesus. I figured I knew about him, but it wasn't like I could really meet him in person, right? But I soon learned that there is more than one way to know a person.

For a while, especially throughout my teenage years, I thought I had everything figured out. I had found a home in karate and with music. I had my plan of what I was going to do in my life, and by all outward appearances, it seemed like I was doing well. But I was still restless, searching for something deeper, something that wasn't dependent on how well I performed or what I could do. During my senior year of high school, knowing that I would be attending a public university in the fall, I decided I needed to figure out what I believed in, and that I might as well start with the Catholic Church. So, to the surprise of everyone who knew me, I started going to Mass regularly on Sundays by myself. I shocked my parents most of all, who struggled to figure out why I suddenly had become a regular churchgoer.

It only took a few weeks before I really began to feel something change within myself. Something, or rather someone, was drawing me to church. When I went there, I slowly began to realize that I didn't have to prove myself to anyone. Absolutely anyone could sit down and pray, and no one was checking to see if I had the right answers. I could come just as I was. I was suspicious about this at first; I thought for sure there was some kind of secret club or group, or that maybe all the people I saw at church who were so welcoming were really just faking it. But week after week they were consistent and continued to welcome me and I realized I was free to be myself with them. The people I met at church, especially the other high school students and youth ministers, were sincere in their faith and their love for Jesus and they were kind to me because they wanted to share that faith and Jesus with me. Once I was able to let my guard down and trust that these people at church had no other motive than to share with me, everything became even more beautiful and real; I felt a peace that I had never known before. Each time I went to church for Mass, I wanted to stay there with Jesus afterward. My friends at church would pray with me, and I knew that I had found a community.

At that time, all the things that I had learned *about* Jesus were coming into focus. He was real and wanted me not just to know *about* him but to *know* him. I knew that the peace I felt came from him and I wanted everyone to experience the same joy and peace I was feeling. I knew it wasn't connected to what I had done or earned but that somehow Jesus was generous with his peace and joy and I didn't have to *do* anything to get it; it was a gift from Jesus to me and to everyone, and I wanted to shout it from the rooftop! By that point, I was all in, I wanted to know everything, do everything I could to learn more about Jesus and Catholicism. I embraced every opportunity to expand my knowledge, thinking that everyone that had been going to church their whole life must be so far ahead of me in terms of their theological understanding. It was in those months of learning, of discovering, and really beginning to pray, that I began to meet Jesus, finding that he wasn't just a historical figure who lived two thousand years ago but a person who wanted a relationship with me in the present. It felt like I was reconnecting with an old friend. The deep and lasting joy that this gave me is difficult to put into words, even now, but as a seventeen-year-old, it was almost impossible to describe.

After Mass one Sunday, I felt my relationship with Jesus go to the next level, as there was this palpable sense that Jesus wanted to spend time with me. It came to a point where my desire to learn more things about Jesus evolved into an even deeper desire to spend time with him, like you would spend time with a friend. From there, I began praying in a sort of conversational way. This new mode of praying really changed everything for me. I realized that praying wasn't just repeating memorized prayers like the Our Father or Hail Mary, but instead that it was a conversation in an evolving relationship. Just as I could share an intimate conversation with a close friend, so I could do it with Jesus! At the same time, I was encountering the Word of God, the Bible, in a new way. On so many occasions during that period, I would hear the reading of the Bible at Mass and the words felt like they were coming directly from Jesus to me. This was the sort of relationship that was growing in my heart with Jesus. I had learned enough about him at this point, and now was the time to be with him and let him be with me.

Accompanying all this was a peace and deep joy that I had not encountered before. It was like I had found something I had lost—it filled a void inside of me that I didn't even know was there. At times I was still a bit skeptical. I mean, how could I have attended Catholic school for so many years and been missing this seemingly integral piece of my life? But the consistent factor in it all was Jesus and our deepening relationship. I wondered if other people related to Jesus in the same manner that I now did. How would I find them? I trusted that Jesus would show me the way.

But while I found peace during Mass, I still felt kind of alone in church. I mean, everyone was with their families, especially on Sundays, and I was by myself. As I started attending regularly, the parish's youth minister would try to invite me to different events the group held for high school–age youth, but I always declined. I didn't need to associate with those "crazy for Jesus" kids—the youth group just was too much for me. But one Sunday, an announcement for Eucharistic Adoration with the youth group intrigued me. What I loved the most about attending Mass was receiving the Eucharist in Holy Communion, which Catholics believe is the actual presence of Jesus himself. The moment of Communion at Mass left me with a feeling deep in my gut that I was home, like I was where I belonged. At Eucharistic Adoration, Catholics can come and spend time with Jesus, who is present in the Eucharist. You can bet I was intrigued by this possibility! The only problem was, Adoration happened at the same time as karate, and I was just about to earn my second-degree black belt. Up until now, music and karate had given me my sense of purpose and belonging, and it was no small thing to consider disrupting that. So, I had a choice to make. Unsurprisingly, I chose karate, going on to earn my second-degree black belt, an accomplishment I'm still proud of.

But the Lord was just warming up my heart. He hadn't forgotten about the invitation to Eucharistic Adoration, even if I had. And so it was that I found myself skipping karate on Holy Thursday, a decision that would change my life forever. That night I truly met Jesus in the Eucharist and the things I had begun learning and started seeing in prayer became alive and vibrant. It was as if in that moment someone hit a hyperdrive button and all the pieces came together: my desire to go deeper into the Word of God, the beginnings of my conversational prayer with Jesus, and my need to go to Mass all fit together for me. It was a moment in which nothing else mattered, and after that I wanted more and more time with him.

From there, week after week, I started going to Eucharistic Adoration, staying as long as I could. It was in these moments of Adoration that I learned how to pray. We would sing songs together and pray for and with each other, all praising and adoring Jesus in the Eucharist. It was in these moments that my relationship with Jesus became real. He was a person I could share all the details of my life with and he cared deeply about everything. In Adoration, I could sit before Jesus and continue to deepen the prayer I had already begun in my relationship with him. Like someone sometimes in the presence of anyone they love, I didn't even have words to say to him most of the time; I just wanted to sit and be with him. It was a place where I knew I was deeply seen, known, and loved in ways that we seldom experience here on earth.

I had been attending Adoration each Thursday for a few months when my birthday came around. I went to church that day, dejected that a close family member hadn't called to wish me happy birthday. As I was leaving the church and walking to my car, I heard someone behind me yell my name and tell me to wait. A few members of the youth group were there with cupcakes and we had a small birthday celebration. It was one of the best birthday parties I'd ever had.

When I left, I realized that through the simple gesture of sharing store-bought cupcakes in a parking lot, I had found a home in my church youth group. These people hadn't known me for very long, but they cared for me. They were truly living the ideal of love: to will the good of the other. Despite my initial skepticism and detachment, the members of youth group genuinely loved me in a way that was different from any type of love I had ever known. They saw me and reflected to me the love that I was beginning to feel Jesus had for me. After that experience of the love of Christ through my church friends in the parking lot, I was forever changed. Again.

Home at Last

You know how my story ends, so you may be surprised to know that despite growing up Catholic, I had really never encountered religious sisters before spending time in youth group. Of course, I had heard about nuns, from pop culture references and people like Mother Teresa. But I didn't think anyone my age still did that—actually became a nun. I had never seen a nun under the age of fifty. I had also always figured that I'd eventually get married to a nice guy, have children, *have a normal life*. I could share my newly rekindled faith with the family that I would eventually have. Right?

The summer after my senior year of high school, I attended a major conference for Catholic youth with thousands of other high school students coming from all over the country and descending upon a college campus for a weekend. It was an amazing weekend of friendship, Eucharistic Adoration and prayer, and praise and worship music. (I'll confess to a weakness for that!) But the thing that really caught my attention was the nuns. Everywhere. And these weren't just older nuns. These were religious women of all ages, of all races and ethnicities, and from different parts of the country. This variety initially shocked me. I had no idea that women like these existed. Seeing them everywhere made me realize something for the first time: this was a path that Jesus could be calling me to journey down. The nuns' presence among us that weekend captivated me. I still didn't know much about religious life, but I knew they lived a life completely for Jesus and their joy was palpable. There was this intuition I had that their life was a life that could fulfill the deep desires of my heart that nothing else seemed to satisfy. Honestly, it scared me in a way, because it seemed too good to be true! I knew that the joy these sisters felt had to have come from Jesus. Could something that good, that beautiful, be his plan for me, too? As strange and scary as it sounded, I knew I needed to explore more.

After the conference ended, I started to immerse myself in learning more about the religious life and signed up to receive informational pamphlets about different orders. I knew I had to begin talking to Jesus about this. I needed to ask him if this was the home that he had been preparing for me all along. But I thought I was still "safe" from ever having to seriously contemplate joining a religious order because initially, all the communities I received information from worked either in the fields of education or health care and I didn't feel that those things were what Jesus was asking me to do. The biggest desires in my heart were to be in a place where I could regularly go to Mass and Adoration and to tell the whole world about Jesus. It was around then that I discovered the Daughters of St. Paul. The first picture I saw of the sisters showed a group of sisters in prayer before the Eucharist, and the second showed a sister holding a video camera! Now, both of those images intrigued me and touched the desires I had deep in my heart. This mission and prayer life spoke to me from the beginning. From the depths of my soul, I knew that I wanted to tell the whole world about the joy and peace that I had discovered through Jesus, and life with the Daughters of St. Paul would allow me to do that.

Having discovered this, I began visiting the Daughters of St. Paul and found so many things resonated within my heart while I was with them. First, the prayer life of the sisters was beautiful and centered around Jesus in the Eucharist. The sisters had daily Mass and, much to my great joy, they got to have an hour of Eucharistic Adoration every day! This hour of Adoration is central to the life of the Daughters of St. Paul. It's called the "Visit" with Jesus as it acts as a visit between dear friends, between Jesus and his bride. It is where the sisters spend time with Jesus and receive the grace necessary to carry out his mission and are able to bring to him all the intentions entrusted to them. The daily one-on-one personal time with Jesus is what sustains and helps grow the relationship between a sister and Jesus so that she can then give Jesus to the whole world.

After that first visit to the sisters, I knew I had to have some serious conversations with Jesus. I was attending college, so I would take time during my breaks from school to attend retreats the sisters had for women who were thinking of becoming sisters. And with each visit I felt more and more at home. Over the span of a few years I got to know the sisters more and they got to know me. I realized that the deep desires of my heart could find their answer in this community of sisters. The desire to live intimately with Jesus, and to tell the world about Jesus, could be carried out through the sisters' mission. After all, the Daughters of St. Paul are tasked with spreading the love of Jesus through media. And they did it creatively! Remember the picture I saw of the sister with the video camera? The reason she had it was because she is a member of the video department filming all kinds of things to help people grow closer to Jesus.

During my senior year of college, I began the formal application process. The application process in itself is quite a journey, but that could be a whole other chapter! The sisters and I both discerned that I could enter after graduation. I graduated from college in May and that August I flew from Texas to Boston to begin this new journey of discovering if this was the home Jesus had been preparing for me all along. Now, one doesn't enter into religious life and that's it, the decision is made. It's more like there are steps that take you deeper and deeper into prayer and knowledge of where Jesus is calling you. The Daughters of St. Paul generally have two years of postulancy, followed by two years of novitiate, and then you make your first vows. Then, after six more years, you make your final vows, which is your yes to Jesus forever!

With each step, there's a lot of praying and a lot of learning. Different sisters help along the way to see if this is where Jesus is calling us to give ourselves completely. Each year until final vows there are evaluations and times of deep prayer where the young women and the sisters can be honest and open in discussing if the Daughters of St. Paul is the place for them to be the most fulfilled. While there were difficulties along the way and times when I wondered if this was really the best place for me, each time I spoke with the sisters, and most importantly, when I spoke to Jesus, I felt more and more that my home was with Jesus in the Daughters of St. Paul. It was such a joy to share this publicly when I had the opportunity to make my final vows in my hometown, at the church where I had discovered Jesus so many years before. It was such a grace to have this beautiful Mass with so many people who had known me from the beginning of my journey home.

My Forever Home

You're probably assuming that now that I've found my home, there's no more circuitous journeying to undertake, that I am settled. Well, since I've made my vows, I've moved over ten times, so sometimes when people ask me where I'm from, where my home is, I have to ask a few clarifying follow-up questions to be able to give them the answer they're looking for. Do they mean where I grew up, or where I live right now, or where I have spent the most time, or where I return for the holidays? Because none of these is really the place I call home. My home is my identity as a child of God, and from the moment of my baptism that identity extends to my life and call as a sister, as the beloved of Jesus. It is the way that Jesus has prepared for me; it is where I feel truly known, and truly loved. And when I look back I can see that Jesus was with me and continues to be with me every step of the way.

But I'll let you in on a little secret: I'm still on the journey, Jesus isn't done with me yet! And he won't be until he calls me to my true forever home, with him after my death. When I will be united with him completely in heaven, as that is the true home to which he is calling each of us. My heart has found the greatest peace and deep joy, deeper than the suffering and sorrow that is part of every life, in continually discovering my home in him. But for me and for each one of us, the longing for home will always remain. Our hearts, as Saint Augustine said, are restless. They won't be fully satisfied until they're filled by an infinite and eternal love—a love Jesus wants to pour into each of them. We're all on this journey home together. My prayer for you is that my journey might inspire you to see how Jesus has been present in your journey all along. Jesus is with us, he has prepared a place for each of us, and the journey with him is one we could never imagine taking on our own.

LOVE IS FIERCER
THAN DEATH

SR. MARIA KIM-NGÂN BÙI, FSP

I felt truly seen and known for the first time when kneeling in front of a golden stand holding a small white host. I was fourteen, my life was a hot mess, and I felt like I had fumbled my way to that weekend retreat. I could not perceive it then, but God began the healing lesson of a lifetime that night.

I hardly knew anyone on the retreat except my older brother. My two brothers, cousins, and I always have been close. I guess it's because we were born to refugees of the Vietnam War, and it took an "all hands on deck" approach to make things happen in our house. My mother was very devout, and my father was very strict. At that point in our family's life, my parents were probably glad to send their two angsty teenagers on a Catholic youth retreat because they were hoping for some help. Until that weekend retreat,

I had spent a few years hanging around a group of teenagers whom I would describe as "edgy." Some of my friends from these years ended up in juvi and others became young mothers. I was unaware that I was desperately searching for meaning. I doubted God's existence and whether it even mattered. *If God exists, why is there so much darkness, suffering, and cruelty in the world?* At least my edgy friends were consistent and authentic. Since there seemed to us to be no order, no purpose to existence, we naturally tested what we saw as arbitrary boundaries.

But somehow the people on this youth retreat seemed even *more* authentic than my edgy friends. *But how? Isn't being religious stifling and boring?* I wondered what made them joyful yet grounded, confident but not arrogant. I wondered what made them think life was so good and whether they were as good as they seemed. I also sensed everyone really respected the youth minister, and since respect from teenagers is hard-earned, I watched him intently. He was disarmingly good and cheerful, and in his presence, you couldn't help but feel loved and welcomed. I had never met anyone quite like this before. So, when he asked us to kneel in front of that golden stand holding a white host and told us it was Jesus, I listened. He said that if we had never met Jesus Christ in a personal encounter, we should ask him for one right then and there.

I will never forget kneeling on the bare open floor of that large cabin in northern Arizona. There were one hundred other teenagers. The room was still, heavy with meaning. The gentle guitar strum underscored the permeating feeling of reverence and solemnity. I took a deep breath, looked at that host, and asked, *Jesus. If you are real. Tell me.* I heard his response in the core of my being almost as soon as the prayer rose from my dark, confused heart. In a moment of inexpressible clarity, Jesus told me he was real, that he loved me, and that my parents loved me more than anyone this side of heaven. Each truth pierced my heart. I felt known, loved beyond words.

Starting that day I have begun to see a pattern in my life. I've noticed that God is always ready to meet me in my brokenness, and that he wants to and can heal me. He's made my life into an adventure because he is constantly taking me deeper and higher and broader than I ever could imagine. I know people say God works with our free will and we need to become open to hear him speak. "He's not rude," they say. "He waits to be invited." But they don't always mention to you how powerful he is in his gentleness. God kicked down a door to come get me. It doesn't sound polite, but that's how God works, at least with me. He waits for our permission, but he will abolish obstacles if we let him.

The more I experience this pattern of his goodness, the more I am convinced it takes courage to allow ourselves to encounter God. His unbounded mercy and goodness are always surprising, always unfathomable. This is why I am convinced that God is and was always there in my life—even when I look back on deep suffering—and he is unafraid to write straight within the crooked and even mangled lines. This light in darkness, this enduring goodness, was a healing balm and has truly been the golden thread through the adventure of my life.

I am a driven person who tenaciously strives for excellence, consistency, reliability, and transparency. Despite how annoying these traits may be at times to other people—not to mention me— there's not much that I can do to change them. It's my character. In junior high, I was friendly with all kinds of kids: the artsy ones from choir and orchestra, the nerds from honors classes, and the edgy kids who were regularly put on probation or expelled. But because I wanted consistency and truthfulness, my "skater" and "stoner" friends were my favorite people. They didn't compete with me in some backhanded, complicated way. No, they professed to not care about most things, and they acted like it. Those years were dotted with risky behaviors that punctuated my search for meaning. They could have sent my life in a whole different direction if I hadn't gone to that youth retreat where I found God; or rather, where I let him find me. Within that little host was an authenticity, a Presence, so true that it ordered the cosmos. Truth found me.

Life did not miraculously get easy after my encounter with Jesus Christ at that retreat. I had to tear myself away from my closest groups of friends as a result of it. But I was determined to figure out how to live in the Truth, with the One who is Love who had found me. I knew that I was too weak to hang around friends who were not orienting their lives toward God. Amid the difficult changes that I made, I felt God giving me the inspiration and courage to pursue him.

I sought truth like I was parched.

God spoke using my love for music during this season of change. I learned that worshiping God through music is a potent way for me to pray. It pierces through troubles and even loneliness, and it unites our souls with the truth that life, and all its grit, is beautiful and good with God.

As a religious sister—consecrated completely to God with vows of chastity, poverty, and obedience—I continue to discover how God wants me to live in reality. It takes courage to be authentic and not to hide the truth of myself from both myself and God. But he continually shows me how he especially wants to heal and revive the areas of my heart that I would rather hide: the places that feel broken, dark, selfish, egotistical, mean. It is freeing to discover again and again that God doesn't abide with inauthenticity. I *say* that I don't like inauthenticity and falseness—everyone does. But the difference between God and us is that he truly, thoroughly, unwaveringly, eternally does not abide with it. The spiritual life for me has been the always new adventure of allowing God to roll up his sleeves and to work on transforming my mind, will, and heart.

Religious Life Is an Adventure

I am willing to bet a lot of people think that life as a religious sister is rather boring. A priest I knew once noted that the three vows that religious sisters, brothers, and priests take are like saying for the rest of your life, "No money. No honey. And you are never the boss." *No money* is the vow of Poverty. *No honey* is the vow of Chastity. *You are never the boss* is the vow of Obedience. So, of course people who are not professed religious would rightly wonder what a person would do for fun if they didn't have disposable income, a lover, and complete independence. But one way I cut through this notion of boredom is to simply invite people to imagine what it would be like to be living with your mom, your sisters-in-law, your sisters, and your girl cousins all day, every day. And you have to share everything.

It's never boring.

In fact, it underscores the essential paradox of life in Christ: you have to let go in order to receive; you have to "take up your cross and follow [Jesus]" if you want to be a true disciple (Luke 9:23).

It was the grit, this willingness to embrace the paradoxes, that drew me to my particular religious order, the Daughters of Saint Paul. We are the spiritual daughters of the man who said, "I count everything as garbage except to know Christ my Lord" (Philippians 3:8) and "[in Christ] power is made perfect in weakness" (2 Corinthians 12:9). The implications of our life are huge and very small at the same time. It's the meeting of the almighty God with his limited creatures. It's our story of love.

The Call to Religious Life

After I met the Lord in that Arizona cabin, I knew I had a lot to learn about the Faith. I had grown up Catholic. My family prayed a rosary every day, went to Sunday Mass, and my mom catechized us better than a religious education class ever could. But because religion was not emphasized or taught at public school, I thought it must not be that important and that it was mostly particular to my family. After my conversion experience, I became deeply aware of how connected everything really is, and I fell in love with what I call "the intellectual backbone of the Church." I asked tons of questions at youth group and listened intently. I started to go to daily Mass and sought out any Catholic spiritual reading I could find. I was enthralled with the beauty of the Church's unwavering moral teachings that follow from our belief in the infinite value of every human made in the image and likeness of God. Because Jesus died on the Cross for us, our lives have a value we cannot begin to fathom. Nothing would or even could ever be the same for me after my conversion.

I received my call to religious life through the intercession of Our Blessed Mother Mary. It began at the end of that retreat when one of the teens held up a book and invited anyone who wanted to join him to make a thirty-three-day preparation for total consecration to the Blessed Mother. He explained about how powerful this devotion can be in leading us deeper into relationship with God. With my heart aflame from my encounter with Love himself, I took a copy of the book and started reading. Those thirty-three days were like intense training. I learned how to pray the rosary and other prayers in English that I only knew in Vietnamese. I learned how to make time for prayer every day and how difficult it is to discipline oneself to be faithful to prayer.

I will never forget the evening when I was kneeling in front of our family's altar praying the rosary. I was praying the Hail Mary while looking at a statue we had of Our Lady of Fatima. I felt enfolded in her gentle guidance and in her beautiful example of openness and obedience to God. When I got to the words "blessed is the fruit of your womb, Jesus," I felt the Blessed Mother draw my eyes to a small statue of the Sacred Heart of Jesus. He was looking directly at me with a strong gaze and his arms held out, completely open. In the center of his chest was a small flaming heart wrapped with the crown of thorns. In that moment, I felt Jesus' immense love for me, like I did that night on retreat, and my eyes flooded with tears of joy. I then heard him ask me the question that has come to shape my life: "Would you give your life to me so that others may know the joy you feel in this moment?" I was stunned. I thought immediately of my friends who were living in such darkness, and I wanted them to know how much they were worth and how infinitely they were loved. So I told the Lord, "Yes, but you have to do everything. You can do everything because you are God." Somehow, I knew that the way to fulfill this request meant becoming a sister, or a nun in popular parlance, and this was a problem. I didn't know any sisters. The only sisters I knew were the ones who sang with Julie Andrews in *The Sound of Music*.

Meeting the First Daughter

The first Daughter of St. Paul I met was a tiny sister whose presence could fill a room, Sister Carmen Christi. She radiated life and joy but was so humble and unassuming that people could not resist wanting to know what made her shimmer. She was on fire. (Sr. Carmen Christi would later become a mentor for me, guiding me through my years of discernment.) I definitely would not have been able to articulate my attraction to the Daughters of St. Paul then, but after saying yes to this life every day for years, I can say that not only is it the grit—the "all in" for Jesus that is at the heart of every Daughter of St. Paul—but it's also the everyday, unassuming boldness to give the raw stuff of life to him over and over again.

A few months after meeting Sr. Carmen Christi, I drove with some girls from youth group to visit one of the Daughters' communities in Culver City, California, for a "Come and See Weekend." This was where my journey with the sisters truly began. Those few days were a great introduction to the tone and character of the community. I spent the time soaking it all in. I watched the sisters with hawk eyes and marveled at their genuine joy.

I had supper that first night squished at a long table with all the sisters. I was so interested in everything happening around me that I ate pretty slowly. I was still finishing the main course as some of the sisters started in on their dessert: Jell-O. And I noticed everyone began taking slower and slower bites. Something was up.

Suddenly one of the sisters broke the silence, declaring, "Oh, don't eat it." She laughed, "It's awful!" Everyone released their spoons, and the feeling of relief gave way to laughter. "What did you do?!" another sister jokingly asked. "We didn't have normal Jell-O, so I took the clear stuff that was donated and added peppermint." Another round of laughter. "And how much peppermint did you add?" More roaring laughter. It was clear that dinner was over.

Then it was time for the evening's recreation, and my friends and I watched as the sisters all flurried about. Some cleared dishes, others began the washing, another wiped the table, while others put the leftovers away. The rest of the sisters moved the furniture to create a large open space. Then the music started. And then the line dancing began. Let's just say I am at best apprehensive about dancing. It's not my forte. But seeing the sisters' simplicity and fun helped me join in. There was a lot of laughter and a few near collisions. I still smile at my photos of the conga line. As the night was winding down, I realized that I was so enjoying the sisters that a couple hours had gone by without my realizing.

The next day my friends and I attended Mass with the community, prayed with them, and listened to a presentation. We went with two sisters, Sr. Carmen Christi and Sister Helena Raphael, to the beach for lunch. I was fascinated because the sisters wore their full habits and sat on a blanket in the middle of the beach as if it were an everyday thing. When other beachgoers looked at us, the sisters simply greeted them with genuine smiles. I was fascinated that they did this so naturally and without interrupting our conversation. I was also intrigued by how very different the sisters were. The one that flitted about, Sr. Carmen Christi, was profound, kind, sweet, and measured, while Sr. Helena Raphael spoke at a California clip, was excited about everything, and wore her kindness in a genuine, bouncy way.

How different the two sisters were was soon comically on display as seagulls suddenly flocked down en masse. The sisters had completely opposite and spontaneously strong reactions. Petite Sr. Carmen Christi screamed and waved her hands desperately while Sr. Helena Raphael looked excited and turned to tell us quickly how she loved birds. It looked like she wanted to feed them. "No!" Sr. Carmen Christi pleaded. "They will not hurt you," Sr. Helena Raphael said; she seemed in awe of the rather persistent birds. We were in stitches.

That was my introduction to community life. I will never forget the tremendous joy, the peppermint-flavored Jell-O, the conga line, the seagulls, and a hodgepodge of other memorable moments that spoke volumes about the joyful life the sisters led.

On the drive back, my friends and I spoke about how happy the sisters were and how unexpectedly fun our time with them had been. The sisters were all utterly themselves, yet singularly devoted to their mission and their God.

I later learned that part of the foundational years of the Daughters involved our cofoundress, Venerable Mother Thecla Merlo, encouraging the sisters to cultivate a "family spirit" within community, which meant being simple, humble, open, hardworking, and very prayerful. Ultimately, it was this no-frills love for God, each other, God's people, the mission, and their prayer that was so attractive to me.

Hiding from the Vocation Director

Despite my yearning to learn everything about the Faith and my growing sense that religious life might be my calling, I was reluctant to speak with the vocation director for the Daughters. The vocation director is a sister responsible for accompanying young women through the process of discerning what vocation God is calling them to and whether God might be calling them to be Daughters of St. Paul. I spoke with her every so often. It was wonderful to have someone who understood my crazy desire to give *everything* to God and to love him unreservedly. She helped me to articulate and understand my prayer experiences and was one of the few people who could understand how Jesus and the Faith were the most precious thing to me.

But I would still get nervous when she called. I felt like she was too good, and I was so far from being even close to worthy to be a religious sister. A few times when caller ID showed *Daughters of St. Paul*, I let other family members pick up the phone and I would insist they say I wasn't home. I even ran outside so when they said I wasn't there it would be true. My mom eventually convinced me that I should at least be polite to the sister and answer the phone.

College or the Convent

The Daughters continued coming to my youth group to speak once a year or so, and I paid close attention to what they said. After they spoke, my friends and I would gather around the sisters to ask questions and to enjoy their fun presence. I remember when one of my friends asked the sisters how sure you had to be before you applied to enter the convent. It was a brilliant and courageous question, one that the rest of us had been too nervous to pose. The question was posed to Sr. Helena Raphael. And true to form, she was quick. *Too quick*, I thought. "I would say about eighty percent sure," she said. I was stunned. *Really?* I thought. *Only 80 percent?!* That meant that you had a 20 percent chance of being wrong—while selling or giving away all your stuff, moving away from family and friends, and going to live with women who were essentially strangers. That sounded like a crazy gamble. But my next thought was, *Oh no.* I was pretty sure I was at 80 percent.

I consoled myself with the fact that I still had two more years of high school before I needed to make a choice.

Junior year was stressful. It was the most important year for any future college plans I might have, and grades and standardized scores really mattered. But I had another layer in my life that no school papers addressed, no scholarships would cover, and it gave no AP credit. *Am I called to be a sister?* Youth group, Mass, or anytime at prayer and spiritual reading were my solace away from all the other craziness.

Thankfully, the hard work paid off, and during my senior year,

I was awarded a full-tuition scholarship, plus room and board, to in-state schools. I received a number of other scholarships, and I planned to use them to cover the many other expenses. My parents were proud, and I was relieved. But despite the good news, my heart was still restless.

I realized that I needed to go visit the sisters one last time before I made the decision about what to do after high school. The Daughters of St. Paul have an annual Holy Week retreat, and so I decided to hop on a plane to Boston, miss a few days of school, and visit the sisters one last time.

When I arrived at the motherhouse in Boston, I was greeted with that now-familiar sense of peaceful joy and openness. I didn't know it then, but I was already starting to truly love the community. The sisters knew me by name, and we had beautiful conversations. But I felt a strange tension: I had worked so hard to get scholarships, yet I had an attraction that could not be shaken. The beauty of giving my life to God, although I knew it would be difficult in ways I could not even begin to imagine, was still more exciting and attractive than the thought of decorating a dorm room with one of my best friends or having college adventures.

I'm Not Good Enough

In addition to all the uncertainty about the next chapter of life, I was still battling the feeling that I was *way* too imperfect and sinful

174

to be a sister. But I had a moment of undeniable clarity and affirmation while reading a biography of Daughters of St. Paul cofounder, Blessed James Alberione. I completely related to the description of complaints from young members of the Pauline institutes who argued it was impossible to live the intensity of the Pauline life, that its intense prayer, study, and work were not sustainable. I found myself moved to tears by Blessed Alberione's response, as I discovered he and I shared the same heart, the same charism.

He told the young Paulines that he would not reduce the time allotted for prayer or study or work because our mission—preaching the Gospel through media—required excellence in each of these areas. All of those hours of prayer, study, and work are needed to know God well in order to give him to others. He reconfirmed them in the ideal of offering the urgent and saving message of the Gospel in the most beautiful way possible. And therefore, he gave what has become known as the Pact, or the Secret of Success. This is a prayer where God and Paulines make promises to each other. Paulines promise and commit ourselves to do everything and to use everything—our poverty of mind, will, heart, time, resources, holiness—for the sake of the glory of God and peace to humanity. God in turn promises to give us everything we need to be faithful, to multiply his gifts abundantly so that our efforts, however lacking, will abound with fruit and grace. It's a promise only God could make, and it's the only thing that made religious life seem remotely possible for me. God could be God—all-powerful, eternally provident. I could be me—limited but with good intentions; offering everything I had for him to bless and multiply for his beloved people.

Discovering the Pact was a moment of profound clarity; I could finally see how I would fit into the Daughters' life. The essence of Pauline life was humility and faith.

It was like the Founder was saying, "Don't look at yourself! Don't think that *you* need to do it because God promises to be with us, and he is almighty and can do everything."

I somehow recognized in the depths of my being that this was God's answer to my feeling of inadequacy. Blessed Alberione knew how unworthy those called to this life would feel, but he knew we were meant to proceed anyway. I soaked in this prayer for a long time, and discovered I knew Alberione's heart and he knew mine. In fact, the musician in me sensed that he and I were not only singing in the same key; we were the same note. I was a barely audible G on the treble clef and Alberione was a G at the end of a huge crescendo. I felt like it was God's way of telling me I could do this.

The Application

A couple days before I was supposed to fly back home to Phoenix, the vocation director asked me where I was at in my discernment. She gently asked me if I still had the desire to enter religious life right out of high school. The truth tumbled out of my mouth, "I didn't know if you all would accept me if I applied." That's exactly what had been keeping me back. I had to admit to myself on that Holy Week retreat that college had become my "just in case" project throughout high school. I knew that the sisters send women in formation through school, so whether or not I would get my degree wasn't a problem.

The sister smiled with warmth and reassurance. She tilted her head a bit and said, "Apply." With that one word, I was flooded with peace, excitement, and joy.

I went straight to a little chapel and knelt right before the tabernacle. Then reality flooded in. My heart sank as I thought about my parents. I pleaded with God. My mom would be supportive of pretty much anything I decided to do, but I knew my father was pretty opposed to my entering the convent. Over the years, I had tried to drop hints, and although he paid for my plane tickets to go see the sisters, he told my brothers and me that we weren't allowed to talk about doing anything with our lives until after college. His stance was clear. So, I had kept my dreams a secret. It was painful to think of how my father might react. I cried in that little chapel asking God to give me the courage to enter and to give my parents grace to understand.

When I left the chapel, I immediately called my dad and told him my decision in the gentlest way I could. He was quiet. I don't think I breathed as I waited for him to respond. After a while he said that he and my mom would have to come out for a visit. Somehow, I refrained from screaming my excitement into the phone. The next plane ticket to Boston would be for my parents, too.

They Understood

For the first step of the application process, I was asked to write my autobiography, and was told I needed to return to Boston to take psychological tests and have interviews with a few sisters.

I went back to Boston a few days ahead of my parents. I didn't mind the tests and interviews and was happy to answer any questions people asked. I was more concerned about how my parents would react to the sisters and the huge convent. My father was friendly but quiet as he met the sisters, and my mom followed his cues. He was deep in thought. One of the few times he spoke was when he saw that the sisters ran printing presses and had bindery equipment. He was impressed because he owns a printing company and remarked how the sisters took care to purchase good machines and ran them well. The rhythm and smell of the printing presses had always evoked home to me and I was glad my father saw the sisters' dedication and care in mission. At a dinner near the end of our visit, my father finally broke his silence and declared to one of the sisters sitting with us, "Well, I'm happy Kim has chosen a good community"—although I wanted my dad to understand that I felt more like God had chosen this place for me—and I felt completely relieved. Both my parents supported me from that moment on.

Recalling the reactions that came from other people back home makes me chuckle a bit now. There were many furrowed brows, pursed lips, awkward silences, and expressions of surprise. I remember one of my teachers asked a friend of mine, "Well, what do you think? Is she going to make it?" My friend smiled and said, "I think so. She's pretty stubborn and she usually finishes the stuff she starts." It was my turn to be surprised because I really didn't know if I would stay. I only knew that God was calling me to enter.

Learning to Be a Daughter

I soon learned what extreme homesickness and excitement mixed with peace feels like. That's pretty much what I remember about my three years in postulancy. There were classes about all the basic things: catechism, communication skills, different flavors of "how to pray," Pauline charism, etc. I have memories of awkward moments learning how to live with many other women. Growing up with brothers never taught me that arguing with women means tension that sometimes lasts two weeks.

It was both fascinating and challenging to learn to live and work so closely with women who were the type that could be determined enough to do something as bold as entering a convent in the new millennium. There were sometimes explosions, but we'll call them fireworks; we sisters like to keep things positive—it is a convent, after all. I learned so much during those three years of postulancy, and I had the incredible opportunity of living with amazingly big-hearted, dedicated women from different parts of the country, and even some from around the world.

There are two built-in, decisive, defining moments each year during postulancy, novitiate (a two-year preparation to profess temporary vows), and temporary vows (or "juniorate," a five- to nine-year period when the sister renews her temporary vows annually). The first moment is the period of time when each woman in formation looks back over the year to pray and think about what she has learned and how she has grown, and to identify areas for further growth. During that time, the young woman and the sisters in charge of formation, who serve as representatives of the community, pray and discern whether God is calling her to move on to the next year. It's a moment of intense honesty and vulnerability. The feedback you receive from the sister who is your "formator," or your mentor and teacher, is given in a spirit of love and prayer. St. Paul tells us to "build one another up" (1 Thessalonians 5:11) and "outdo one another in showing honor" (Romans 12:10). And so, this time can be a moment of gratitude and encouragement, even if it means facing yourself starkly.

The other decisive moment is when the young woman returns from visiting family for a few weeks. It was always hard for me to go back to the convent because it meant leaving the people I loved so much. Saying goodbye to my parents at the airport is the only memory I have of my dad crying. But it was also a moment to reconfirm my love for the Lord and to make a purposeful decision. In sister-speak, these are moments of "saying yes." Although these yeses cost something, I treasure them because they are opportunities to make deeper choices.

Novitiate is a special time in the life of any religious. Novitiate within the Daughters of St. Paul is a two-year process. The first year is usually what is called the canonical year. It's a year of preparation for vows, required by canon law. During this year, the novice cannot miss more than fifteen days of novitiate without making them up, and she will have to repeat the year if she misses more than three months. It is meant to be an intensely spiritual and humanly formative time. The entrance into novitiate even has a special, formal ritual given by the Church, called Rite of Entrance into Novitiate. Once that ceremony is completed, the novice is considered a member of the community and is addressed as "Sister." It took me a while before I responded to "Sister." I always hoped people didn't think I was being rude when I seemed to ignore them.

I learned a ton as a novice, and a lot of that wisdom came from my novice formator. A sister's relationship with her novice formator is something that shapes the rest of her religious life. The novice formator is like the dean, one of the professors, and your spiritual mentor for a two-year intensive course—like spiritual boot camp—that attempts to help you get to the core of who you are so that you can make a total, free, joyful gift of your life as a religious sister forever. She sees your best and your worst over the course of your time together because there are a lot of ups and downs in the journey to profession.

My novice formator, Sister Karen Marie, was tall, funny, fun-loving, joyful, perceptive, and had a smile that seemed to say, "I see you. I believe in your goodness and your potential even more deeply than you can see for yourself. You are God's beloved daughter."

Going into that year, I had doubts as to whether I could really live the life: poverty, chastity, obedience, community life, the apostolate. Those are big words. We were told that obedience was the hardest vow, and as a young novice, it is hard to understand what you haven't lived. Having lived it, I think obedience is hard in large part because the superiors do not have the time, brain space, or ability to reason and walk with each sister when she accepts new assignments or new roles in the apostolate. Novitiate is meant to prepare you for many of those challenges and joys of religious life.

During the second year of novitiate, the young woman is sent to a small community to spend about six months "trying on" the life as she would if she were a professed sister. The novice sees and experiences what living poverty, chastity, and obedience is in real time and in real situations. We call this an apostolic experience. It is another chapter in the adventure of becoming a sister. I was ready to love the sisters in my small community of four and I was ready to try everything. But I asked a lot of questions, and even though the sisters teased me a bit about it, I still asked my questions because in taking these vows I was about to make a bet with my life.

Near the end of novitiate, we pray long and hard to discern before writing a letter to be admitted to the next step in formation: First Profession or temporary profession. During that time, we are encouraged to pray about what name we would like to take as a vowed religious sister.

I always loved the idea of names. Names carry meaning and

have pivotal significance in sacred Scripture. In my family, names are chosen with much care and have layers of meaning. My given name, Kim-Ngân, means something like "precious wealth" in Vietnamese and I was baptized Maria Magdalena. I thought "Magdalena Kim-Ngân" might be a nice-sounding name, but when I asked God what name he called me, I felt a gentle warm response in my heart that said "Maria Kim-Ngân." Well, I couldn't argue with that.

Professing the Vows

I made First Profession of vows as a Daughter of St. Paul five years after I entered. That day was unforgettable, and I had adrenaline coursing through my veins so much that I could hear my pulse in my ear. It was one of the happiest days of my life. Whereas the entrance into novitiate is a private ceremony in the community, loved ones and friends are invited to attend a profession. It was the first time many of my friends and family had ever been inside a convent. They were happy for me and they were able to witness me take a huge step in my life.

As much as postulancy and novitiate were adventures, my six years of juniorate, or temporary profession, were more difficult and amazing than I could have imagined.

I first noticed that something had changed after First Profession when I was hustling through an airport to get to the next gate. At a certain point I realized that I felt irritated because people were staring at me, and I could not understand why. It felt pretty rude. When I finally looked down to put my backpack on the ground, I remembered that I was wearing a habit. *Kim*, I said to myself, *you would have stared, too.*

My first assignment was in northeast Philadelphia, where I served for three years coordinating our book and media evangelization at parishes and conventions and promotional activities for our local Pauline Books and Media Center. I was then asked to transfer back to our community in Boston, where I studied business and marketing at Boston College, and helped launch a new national apostolic initiative for the Daughters called JClub Catholic Book Fairs, which are like Scholastic Book Fairs but for Catholic schools. I had to learn a bit of HTML coding to migrate a website, principles of design and production of a magazine, how to navigate customer service to people all over the country, how to work in a publishing house, and so much more. Initially, I did not want to study marketing. I was afraid it was a superficial and manipulative field. But I have grown to love it, and it has since become my full-time apostolate. I found that good marketing is about speaking the truth so clearly and succinctly that onlookers can't help but glance at a thing you made and understand how your mission is about making their lives a little better, or in our case, letting them know how much they are loved by God. I love the people we work with, and I love the challenge of collaborating in a team working with tight resources. It takes creativity, intelligence, and heaps of grace to do it well. At the beginning and end of every day, I try to surrender everything into

Our Blessed Mother's and God's hands and tell him that he is the boss. I ask him to make and show the way forward, and he does.

Love Fiercer Than Death

Throughout formation, especially juniorate, we are encouraged to be totally authentic with ourselves and with others. I tried to live as faithfully as possible in my new life as a professed sister. There was so much to learn, and so many layers to true authenticity.

I felt in my bones that I was called to be a daughter of Alberione and a Daughter of St. Paul. But there were many moments when situations converged, and I questioned whether or not I could do this thing called religious life for the rest of my life. It was never just one thing, but usually a combination of dozens of little factors that made me pray and consider this question for days or even weeks on end. It was the tension of whether or not I had the interior strength or if I truly desired to say yes to this life even if it meant that I might not be able to travel home for every special event in my family's life; even if it meant I might feel at times misunderstood or lonely; even if it meant belonging to and being deeply identified with a Church that is so broken and whose leaders are sometimes willfully blind, selfish, and sinful; even if the decisions of sisters in leadership did not seem to make sense and I had to follow anyway; even if it meant I could not have my own family and children, ever. These kinds of questions still make me pause sometimes even after years in community. And that question about the horrendous duplicity of leaders in the wider Church still stings and throbs like an open wound that may never fully heal.

It's strange to reflect on these doubts because I've grown accustomed to saying, "God sees everything." I used to feel like trusting in God was like a free fall—a sudden, rapid descent into an oblivion of things out of my control. But I had discovered that trusting in God, however risky it feels, usually ends in my rediscovering how unfathomably personal, caring, and intimately provident his love is. Trusting God feels more like stepping into the embrace of One who is better and kinder than I expect. It is always surprising, but always good. So, I often say humble, little prayers like, *I want to do only and always your will. Teach me.* He outdoes my hopes and fulfills even those desires that are so deep that I can hardly face them. He gives inexpressible happiness.

He was not kidding when he said that his joy would be in his disciples and that our joy would be full (John 15:11). And this joy is unshakable when we hold on to him.

The most powerful experience of this unshakable grace came to me a handful of years ago when I was shattered by a traumatic betrayal. It shook my foundation and it threatened to crumble everything that was holding reality together. As a result, I was plunged into debilitating depression and experienced symptoms of PTSD for over a year.

In coming face-to-face with an indescribable darkness, I also experienced that eternal truth that seems so quiet and subtle: Love conquers death and Light dispels darkness. I discovered the might of God's Love largely through my sisters and others who loved me through this time.

I was loved back to life. It was an experience of community, that profound "family spirit" that will forever be an unwavering beacon for me on the path ahead.

Living Love's Promise

Prayer was difficult in that time—it felt often actually impossible—and it's still challenging sometimes when I am confronted with seemingly insurmountable obstacles or incongruencies and the utter hypocrisy of some people in the Church. I want to pray well, and it can be—especially in the beginning—dry, doubt-ridden, and even desperate when you are interceding for family or friends. God and Our Blessed Mother have gradually taught me how to walk through those arid times. Early on, I learned how healing and grounding it can be to simply stop inside a church to say a few words to the Lord in the Blessed Sacrament. Bit by bit, I have grown familiar with what it feels like to be received and strengthened. I have acquired a taste for that stillness and peace of God's presence and for allowing myself to be loved and made whole. I have discovered anew that the love he promised when he spoke to me on that bare floor in northern Arizona in front of that little white host is truer and more faithful than I can comprehend.

Each day of my religious life has been an unexpectedly beautiful gift. Some days were so hard I thought they would never end, but most days are so fulfilling that I will need eternity to thank God for the tremendous gift of his fierce love in this mysterious, beautiful life with him, his beloved people, and my sisters, the Daughters of St. Paul.

OPEN INVITATION

SR. JULIE MARIE BENEDICTA TURNER, FSP

I was on a video call a while ago with a dear friend, a nonpracticing Catholic. I told her I was working on this project and asked what she would be interested in hearing from a nun her own age.

"I don't know, I guess big-sister stuff? Like, how in the world do you have it all together?"

I stared at her, dumbfounded.

"Oh, shoot! Did FaceTime freeze again?" she mumbled, leaning closer to her laptop.

"No ... I'm just ... You think I have it all together?" I stuttered, eyebrows raised.

"Well, maybe not *you* you, but ... like, as a nun, I guess."

I burst out laughing. "Oh, hon, *me* me is all I've got. Jesus knew exactly what he was getting when he invited me here. The veil might cover up a few warts, but they're still there."

She laughed. "I guess that's true." After pausing, she added, "Actually, that's probably why we're still friends. You're still you."

○

Sometimes, I'm still not really sure *why* Jesus invited me here. What was he thinking? In fact, for about ten years I was pretty sure I had to be making it up, so I ignored it. I was convinced people like me didn't become nuns. Sisters were supposed to be quietly graceful, sweet, subtle, and beautiful, in a classic-but-simple kind of a way. I'm clumsy, outspoken, snarky, and assertive. I have a quick temper, a sweet tooth, and zero patience for doing things for appearances' sake (e.g., I'm convinced fake flowers are an invention of the devil, but I digress). Certainly at least *some* of that would disqualify me, I reasoned. And since I was also very interested in getting married and having a bunch of kids, I didn't mind being disqualified. I ignored the feeling, like a tickle in the back of my heart, that someone was trying to get my attention. Obviously, Jesus did eventually prevail, but it was a long journey to get to that point.

One thing I learned about the Lord in all my procrastination is that when he extends an invitation, he doesn't rescind it. Like Aladdin holding his hand out to Jasmine, asking, "Do you trust me?" he just keeps his hand there, with infinite patience and gentlemanly demeanor, waiting, his eyes gazing with love and warmth and hope, willing to go wherever I need to go, keeping his hand ready for me to notice he's still there and reconsider stepping into a whole new life with him.

But in all reality, it's been a bit of a messy ride. I certainly don't, as my friend suggested, "have it all together," even after eight years of religious life. I don't always answer yes when Jesus holds out his hand or asks for my trust. I'm not always convinced he's paying attention or is ready to catch me when I feel like I'm falling into an abyss. Still, I have been slowly coming to a place where I have to admit—begrudgingly, at times—that he has been present at every moment, using all of my experiences of pain, joy, sorrow, and delight to draw me to him. I'll try to share a few examples to illustrate what I mean.

"I want to be a teacher when I grow up," I declared to my third-grade classmates as I read my essay to them. "I will have at least three dogs, and I will use summer vacations for writing books. My husband will be a writer, too, and we will travel around the world." My classmates applauded politely, and I waited for the requisite question-and-answer session to start.

"What kinds of books will you write?" Sarah asked, her black curly hair bouncing as she raised her hand.

"Funny ones," I said, as though it should be obvious.

"What's your favorite kind of dog?" Miguel asked from the back row.

"Labradors," I answered easily.

"Where in the world do you want to go?" James asked, looking concerned as he pushed his thick glasses higher on his nose. I blushed and paused a second. *He couldn't know he was the writer-husband I was picturing in this scenario, could he?* "Because traveling around the world is pretty expensive," he continued. "You'll probably have to think about that."

"Well . . . um . . . I don't know. I'll have to decide that when I'm grown up, I guess." James nodded, satisfied, as our teacher moved to end the conversation. I returned to my seat, still feeling the warmth in my face.

Apart from James, who was less of a friend and more of a competitor in the challenge to see who could earn more Pizza Hut certificates by reading books from the school library, I really didn't have any friends since my best friend, Kate, had moved away earlier in the year.

No one really talked to me except when we were doing homework in groups. I was a verifiable nerd, and my group nearly always finished first, which meant first dibs on a computer station loaded up with Oregon Trail (my secret goal was always to make sure a character named after the class bully, Brette, got diphtheria or a snakebite before the end). If the computers were taken, my next choice was one of the beanbag chairs in the reading corner, though usually there was less competition for those than for some of the games like Battleship, Connect Four, or Operation. Often James and I ended up getting the reading corner to ourselves, which was perfect as far as I was concerned. I relished the quiet feeling of intimacy that required so little effort.

Eventually James got into sports and started hanging out with the other athletic boys, and I was alone in the corner. I tried to convince myself that was fine, too.

◯

"Julie! Your friend is on the phone!" Mom shouted down the hallway of our mobile home. I put my book down, confused. *Friend? Who could she possibly be talking about? Is she sure it's for me?*

I shuffled my socks across the hollow kitchen floor into the living room and picked up the receiver, curling the cord between my fingers.

"Hello?"

"Hey! It's Maria."

"Oh . . . hi?" I felt my face scrunch up in disbelief. "Maria . . . um, what's up?"

"Hey, have you done the math homework yet?"

Oh. Of course I had. I always did all my homework on the bus if I could so I could have the afternoons free. "Yeah, I did the homework."

"Oh, good! Um, did you get number seven? Because I totally don't get it."

I stretched the phone cord to reach its limit and picked up my backpack. "Hold on, let me check."

"Awesome!"

I took a deep breath and pulled the assignment from my folder. "Yeah. Number seven: 156 divided by 4. Want me to walk you through it?"

"Um, not really. I just kind of need the answer."

"Oh. Okay. I got 36."

"Are you sure?"

No, genius, I put it on my paper because I think it might be wrong. "Pretty sure."

"Okay, cool. What about number nine?"

"How's your friend?" Mom asked as I trudged my way back to my room, dropping my backpack by the front door.

"She's not my friend. She just wanted help on the math homework."

"Friends can call each other for homework help!" Mom seemed a little insulted. She didn't always enjoy school growing up, and probably got some help from time to time herself. "She thought to call *you*, not some other kid. Maybe she *wants* to be friends." She gave me a "gotcha" look and went back to relighting the pilot light on the gas furnace for the fourth time that week.

Okay, maybe she's right, I thought. *I'll give Maria a chance. Maybe tomorrow.* The next morning I waved at Maria as I walked into class and she gave me a little half smile. *At least she didn't totally ignore me. Maybe she does want to be friends?* I allowed myself a little hope. Maybe it was worth a try.

When the bell rang for recess, I caught up with Maria and Emily. They always came as a pair.

"Hey, can I do something with you guys at recess today?" I asked, keeping my tone calm, almost bored. *Can't let them know it will crush me if they say no.* They looked at each other and giggled. "Sure!" Maria answered. "We were just talking about playing hide-and-seek. Sound good?"

I couldn't believe it. They said yes. Might I end the day with a couple of friends? Was it possible?

"Who's it?"

"I'll be it," Emily jumped in. "But the rule is, no hiding together!"

"Okay!" I rushed off to a hiding place as Maria made her way to the other side of the school building. And I waited. And waited. And waited. *This isn't that good of a spot.*

Finally, I peeked between the bushes. Nothing. I crept to the corner of the building and looked around the edge. There they were, Emily braiding Maria's hair as they half hid behind the ramp leading to the computer lab.

They were laughing hysterically about something. I felt a knot forming in my stomach. *Were they laughing at me? Making fun of me for wanting to spend time with them, for thinking maybe I'd want to be friends?*

I swallowed hard and walked toward the ramp. "Hey, did you guys give up?"

They jumped up and took off running. I still didn't want to believe they were just being mean, so I decided they were playing hide-and-seek by a different set of rules. I shrugged and ran after them. I looked everywhere but couldn't find them. Finally, I decided to take a break and go to the girls' room. When I walked in, it looked empty, but I heard whispers from a few stalls down. I'm still not sure why I decided to investigate; I'm sure I already knew what I was going to find. Still, I crouched down. There were no shoes under the door, so I dropped to the ground and looked under. There were Emily and Maria, standing on either side of the toilet seat, leaning against the handrail.

"I found you guys!" I said.

"Are you *still* here?" Maria rolled her eyes. "Can't you take a hint?"

"I mean, seriously." Emily jumped down and unlocked the stall door, nearly smacking me in the face with it. "Look, we'd rather spend time on a *toilet* than spend recess with you. We're leaving. Don't follow us."

"How was your day at school, Jules?" Mom asked when she got home from work that evening.

"It was fine," I lied. "I'm really tired, though, so if anyone calls, could you tell them I can't talk?"

"Sure. You feeling okay?"

"Yeah, just need some quiet time." I lay down on my bed, and after a few minutes, I heard the phone ring, followed by Mom's footsteps coming to my door.

"I know you didn't want to talk to anyone, but your friend says she just needs help with her homework for one minute."

I kept perfectly still, breathing slowly, my book resting on my chest.

"Julie?" Mom whispered. She paused a second, then turned out my light. "Sorry, Maria," I hear her say. "She's just not feeling well. Maybe you could call someone else. . . . Okay. Have a good night." I rolled over toward the wall, tracing the grain on the faux-wood paneling with my finger, and vowed never to care about having friends again.

* * *

About twenty-five years later, I knelt before an altar, one hand on a Bible and the other over my heart, and vowed to live chastity, poverty, and obedience. Most of my family was there, tears in their eyes, telling me how proud they were of me. But what was most moving to me were the seventy-five sisters in the surrounding pews, smiling, singing, and celebrating as I joined their ranks, took on a new name, and publicly stated, "I commit myself to live in communion with my sisters." In making my vows, I was responding to God's love and declaring my love for him. A major part of that journey for me had included falling in love with the sisters of the Daughters of Saint Paul; it was through them that God had not only helped me to believe in and experience his love for me, but had worked several miracles of healing in my heart through their realness.

In the first year after I entered the convent, about three years before I made my first vows, I had gone to the sister in charge of my formation, or training in religious life. Something had been weighing on me, and I knew I needed to share it with her. I was nervous, though, since I was pretty sure that telling her would change things. I thought I might even be asked to leave the convent, and I was prepared for a painful rejection. But I knew if I didn't bring this situation to light and allow it to enter into our mutual discernment about whether God was really calling me, I would never really be sure. More than anything, I wanted to be as certain as possible that I was responding to a genuine invitation and not imposing myself on Jesus or my sisters. So, with a huge knot in my stomach and a few boxes in my bedroom (just in case I needed to start packing that day), I poured out my heart to Sister. She listened, nodded, asked questions, and cried with me until I got to the end of my story. Then came the moment I was sure would be the end of my experiment with religious life. Instead, Sister sat back and let out a slow, deep breath.

"Thank you so much for trusting me with this," she said. "I'm amazed at how obvious God's hand has been through all of your difficulties. And that he would use all of that to bring you here; it's a miracle. It gives me even more love and respect for you, knowing this part of your life." She smiled and pierced me with her gray-blue eyes. "And I can't wait to see how God will use it for his glory."

I was stunned. Never before had I experienced such a positive response to a show of vulnerability on my part, from anyone. In the following weeks, I felt myself begin to settle into the community. I began to see myself as a real member and to feel the freedom to let myself invest in the new relationships I was forming. It wasn't long before I began to realize how much these women meant to me. There is no one in the world I love more than my little brother and sister, and I would never expect those relationships to be supplanted; still, there was something genuinely *sisterly* about the way I felt toward these women. It was almost disconcerting. And in our best moments, I was being appreciated genuinely for who I was rather than for what I could do, which was also a new experience. I had always been the "helpful" one or the "smart" one or the "give it to Julie, she'll take care of it" one, filling roles that weren't really mine to fill. The only expectation I felt here was that I be completely and authentically myself.

I grew up in a mobile home park in the Mojave Desert. A short cinder-block wall at the entrance to the park read "Friendly Village." I have never known a wall more dedicated to the truth, however; much to my family's amusement, the *R* was always falling off, a red-necked Virgil warning Dante of the fiendly nature of what he would find if he embarked upon his intended journey. Yet enter we did, every afternoon after being deposited by the school bus at the curb.

Our trailer was about halfway through the park, a little less than a ten-minute walk from the entrance. For a few years, Mom was always at the bus stop to walk home with my siblings and me. But at some point, she got another job, and my siblings and I had to walk it alone. By the time I was nine, my brother seven, and my little sister five, I was the one shepherding them home, trying to keep them moving and away from other residents. It wasn't a huge trailer park, but it had its fair share of drugs, violence, and other questionably legal activities that shouldn't be witnessed by young children. Our home wasn't really an exception to this, but there was always something worse we could point to and say, "At least we don't have to deal with that." So by comparison, we were fairly normal—and would have been even better off if only Dad wouldn't bring his weirdo friends home so often, sometimes to crash on our living room sofa for weeks at a time, messing the place up and making Dad act even more stupid than usual.

I got good at creatively answering the questions of the nicely dressed people with clipboards who would knock on our door occasionally.

"Those are some pretty big bruises you've got there! How'd that happen?" one overly cheerful lady asked through the screen door after I'd told her Mom was in the shower.

"Oh! Let me show you!" I acted as excited as I could. I grabbed my roller skates and showed them to her. "They were a birthday present! I'm still learning to use them." I laughed. "I guess I'm not very good yet, because I keep crashing." The skates *were* fairly new, but I had been skating for years. That's not where the bruises had come from, but the lady bought it.

"Well, keep practicing!" She laughed, and stuck a business card under the door. "Give this to your mom so she knows I was here, okay?"

"Okay, bye!" I waved. As her car pulled away, I spit my gum into the card, threw it away, and went back to my chores.

As the oldest kid, I helped with homework, packed lunches,

and got good at cooking anything that basically required boiling water: mac and cheese from a box, egg salad, that sort of thing. I'd make dinner when necessary and help with household chores when I felt like it might help keep tempers under control. I could usually tell how the night was going to go by the way Dad's truck pulled into the driveway.

On Saturdays, when Dad was home and Mom had to work, the mobile home was a "no kids allowed" zone. Dad and his friends would lock us out, and we'd spend the day outside. My brother and sister would play with the kids in the neighboring lots, and I would climb a tree and settle in with a pile of books, occasionally picking the lock on the back door if someone needed to use a bathroom.

On Sunday morning, we'd all get dressed and pile into the car for 9:00 a.m. Mass at our local church. I really didn't like church; Mom had to drag me out of bed to get me to go. Apart from just being bored, I didn't like that we were all on our best behavior— Dad included. He sang in the choir and had a great, booming laugh. People there loved him and would always comment on what a lovely family we were. Church became a place of make-believe. We pretended to be smiley, clean-cut, well-behaved kids. Dad pretended to be a doting breadwinner. Mom pretended everything was fine.

Growing up, I don't think I ever really understood why my family went to Mass or what the teachings of the Church were. I was mostly under the impression that it was just what good people did, and that Grandma and Poppa would be really disappointed if we didn't. Sometimes I would sneak a book in with me to pass the time, and if I couldn't do that, I'd count the squares in the ceiling or the shapes in the stained glass windows. It felt like a show, like we were there to be entertained. It didn't help that this particular parish had an affinity for liturgical dance involving tambourines and streamers. But I didn't know any better at the time, so I just decided it was a weird show meant mostly for old people.

It wasn't until much later that I came to realize that I didn't need to put on a show for God, that he was the one I could be the *most* real with. A few years after my conversion, I had a falling-out with a close friend in college. We argued, she called me some cruel names, and my insides ached in a way I didn't know they could. I didn't know who to call; our social circles were too intertwined and I didn't want to ask friends to take sides. I drove around a little and ended up curled in a ball on the floor of the adoration chapel in church. Mercifully, no one else came in for a couple of hours. I sobbed, yelled, accused God of having caused all my problems. There's a scene in the animated movie *Moana*, after the main character's shipwreck, where she kicks at the ocean—the omniscient, omnipotent godlike character—and screams, "Fish pee in you!" I love that scene. I've often shown it in youth group settings, saying, "This is what genuine prayer looks like, sometimes. Sure, at times it's gushy and lovey-dovey, but sometimes it's like this. And that's totally fine; God can take it." That's how my prayer was that day. It was painful having a relationship fall apart in the way that it did; but I came away from the experience with a much deeper relationship with the Lord.

When I finally regained my composure on that chapel floor and tried to listen, I realized that he was with me. Like, really *with* me. Surrounding me, hugging me, filling my heart, and calming me down. I trusted him, knew I could rely on him, and knew that he could handle anything I would throw at him.

When I was a kid, Sunday mornings were a drag. I did, however, love Sunday afternoons and Monday evenings, when Mom would take us to Grandma and Poppa's house. I would sit on the sofa in their living room with Poppa as we watched *Star Trek: The Next Generation* together. My little brother and sister would be playing dress-up with our even littler cousins in the other room, while Mom, Grammy, and my aunties would do crafts in the kitchen.

I lived for those Monday nights. I waited all week for the sanctuary of those hours when "the kids" were all supervised by real adults. It was safe, quiet, and Grammy nearly always busted out the ice cream. Plus, Poppa was the only person who understood me. He liked sci-fi and watched the news and loved to read. And he loved that I loved to read. Everyone else just made fun of me for it.

During a couple of summers when I was a kid, Poppa took me fishing for a few days, just the two of us. We brought granola bars and juice and relied on catching fish and finding berries for the rest of our meals. He taught me the names of wildflowers and which ones were edible, and how to cast my hook into the calm spot in the river behind a large rock where the trout liked to hang out. I remember those trips as the most peaceful and genuinely fun times of my childhood.

Early in the morning on one of these trips, I was reeling in a catch but couldn't quite land it. Poppa hurried over to help, but just as he was taking my rod he slipped on a mossy rock and landed in the water with a shout. I had never heard my grandfather use words like that before, and I covered my mouth to keep from laughing. He pulled in the fish, and it was a tiny little thing, too small to keep. We laughed together until our sides hurt.

That evening, sitting by the campfire and watching the stars, we had an odd conversation. "Julie, I was wondering: What do you think about Jesus?" he asked me.

I really didn't think anything. I shrugged. "I don't know. I guess he seems nice. They talk about him sometimes at CCD, but mostly we just color pages and learn Christmas carols. It's kind of boring."

"Hmm." Poppa rubbed his chin and looked at the stars. "I don't know if a God who can make all of that could be boring. Maybe you ought to give it a little more thought."

I wasn't really interested, but Poppa *had* thrown himself into the creek for my fish that morning, and I hadn't laughed like that in a long time—if ever. The question he asked seemed important to him, so I decided I would try reading a book about Jesus or something.

When I got home, I pulled out the Bible that I had been given for First Communion and started reading at the beginning. It wasn't long before I closed it. *Yep. Just as I thought—boring.* It went into the bottom of the bookcase, and I pulled out another volume of Nancy Drew.

That memory always feels a little like an inside joke between me and God—that I would be so bored by the Bible is kind of hilarious. Now I can't get enough of Scripture. It's the last thing I look at before I go to sleep, and the first thing I read in the morning. It comforts me, challenges me, and brings forth really strong emotions in me.

For example, there's a Gospel story about Jesus sleeping in a boat while a storm rages on—that one gives me all the feels. The disciples finally freak out and wake Jesus up. He takes care of the storm, but then scolds the disciples for not having had enough faith. Sometimes when I read that story, I find myself standing in awe of Jesus, who is sovereign even over the storms. Sometimes I find myself angry with him—"They were scared for their lives, and you're going to chew them out? Seriously?" I know what it's like to not feel safe, to be out of control and convinced this new scary thing is going to be the end of you, and I'm pretty sure I'd have been right there with Peter and John, shaking Jesus awake and screaming at him to make the storm stop.

More and more, though, I'm learning to trust him.

It's true, I know what it's like to be scared out of my mind. But I also know what it is to be protected. I remember hearing my grandfather's voice in our trailer late at night every once in a while, mediating an argument between my parents. I'd try to stay awake and listen, but the volume would always go way down once he arrived. With Poppa there, a strange calm would come over me, and I'd feel safe and fall asleep. I'm slowly learning to trust that, in the moments when I feel like Jesus is sleeping on the job, he's really communicating to me that everything is going to be okay. Looking back, I see that he's allowed some things to happen that were terrible and I don't think I'll ever understand why. But everything that has happened to me has brought me to where I am now, to my community and to a deep relationship with God that I wouldn't change for anything. So even when I don't understand, even when I feel the anger rise in my heart all over again, I can believe that I don't need to try to take control. It's not my job. Maybe I just need to put my head on the pillow next to his and rest with him. If he needs to get up and take care of business, he will.

Just as I was starting middle school, Mom had had enough of our current situation. Dad moved to Washington State and spent a few months in a drug rehab facility while the rest of us moved in with Grandma and Poppa. I wrote Dad a letter only once during this time.

I had included a little handmade gift and my school picture, but the package got returned to me a month later, with *Insufficient Postage* stamped on the envelope. I never tried to resend it. He wrote me a letter, too, in a card with puppies on the front. He said he couldn't wait for us to join him, but I secretly hoped we never would. I didn't want to move, and since we'd been staying with my grandparents, life had gotten a lot more normal. I didn't want to give that up. But Mom had promised my dad that if he could get his act together and hold down a job for six months, we'd move to be with him.

Mom was true to her word, and the day after Christmas and two weeks before my thirteenth birthday, we piled into her Chevy van with a U-Haul trailer attached and drove for two straight days until we got to the northwestern corner of Washington. I was used to not having friends, but now we didn't even have neighbors or cousins or the comfort of my grandparents, and I became the ultimate moody teenager. To make matters worse, we'd left the sunny Mojave Desert and arrived in the Pacific Northwest during the biggest snowstorm the area had seen in a decade. Our U-Haul got stuck a few hundred yards from the house, and we had to trudge through more snow than we'd ever seen in our lives, carrying suitcases and boxes to the front door.

Dad was mostly sober for a few years, but things started getting tough again once I was in high school. I found a part-time job and got involved in every extracurricular activity that held any interest for me at all. I competed in all kinds of arenas, doing research projects and service activities, learning graphic arts and web design, and going to national competitions every summer. I joined the video club, the theater club, the debate team, and earned after-hours privileges in the photo darkroom. In my senior yearbook, I was named "Most Active Senior Girl." I wasn't trying for a record or anything, I just desperately needed to stay occupied and away from home. By that time I had a good group of friends, and when we weren't wrapped up in some competition, musical production, or other project, we'd hold shopping-cart races in the Target parking lot, see how many people we could fit into a vintage VW Bug, or hang out by one of several backyard fire pits available to us.

The day finally came when Mom was driving with me the three hours east to Central Washington University for freshman orientation. We checked out the dorms and sat in on a couple of the information sessions but decided to skip the rest of the programming and went out to lunch.

"Why don't we see if we can find the church closest to campus?" Mom suggested.

"Okay," I agreed. There was no harm in knowing where it was. It didn't mean I had to go—and I wasn't planning to. We checked the phone book outside the restaurant for the address and did our best to map out a route using the street map in the front, but we never did find the church.

A few days into classes, I decided to leave campus and go in search of a grocery store for a few things. It was before smartphones were a thing, and I have a terrible sense of direction, so it shouldn't have been a surprise to me when I got hopelessly lost. I wandered more or less in the direction of campus, when I found a sign hand-painted with bold letters: "Catholic Campus Ministry / BBQ / Free / 3–7pm Today / Everyone Is Welcome." *Well, I'm Catholic, I guess,* I thought, really more interested in the free food and someone to ask for directions. So I went in. I was greeted warmly and given a little tour by a beautiful, well-dressed girl who introduced me to a boy named Mark, who was a year ahead of me and had an infectious laugh that often rose above the conversation.

"Hey, have you been to our Mass on campus?" he asked, tossing me a bag of Cheetos.

"No, there's Mass on campus?" I was a little surprised.

"Yeah! It's at seven p.m. First one of the semester is tomorrow. I'm in the choir." He winked. "We're pretty good. That's a lie; we're okay. But you should come!"

"Um, yeah, sure, okay." I laughed awkwardly, suddenly feeling very shy.

The campus ministry group quickly became my entire social life. There were formal events four nights a week, and informal hangouts almost all the time. There was a chapel in the center, and for the first time in my life, I tried to learn to pray. The weekly Bible studies and casual conversations around theology and philosophy were super interesting to me, and I ended up changing my major. I had started thinking I would become a high school Spanish and literature teacher, but quickly decided teaching wasn't for me. By the beginning of my sophomore year, I had declared a philosophy major and began reading anything I could wrap my head around, and a lot that I couldn't. I also took a position helping to run the campus ministry, which meant I lived on-site for extremely cheap rent.

My parents divorced during my first year away, and while I was glad I didn't have to be around for it, I was concerned for my brother and sister, who were still living at home. By my third year, my dad started calling regularly, asking for help with things, and I could tell he wasn't doing well. When I told him for the third or fourth time that I was a college student living on loans and didn't have any money to send him, he threatened suicide and stopped calling and answering his phone.

Conveniently, this was right around the time of my twenty-first birthday, and I had no shortage of people willing to accompany me to the bars to drink away the stress, sometimes five nights a week. My philosophy studies brought a newfound enlightenment, and God became an unnecessary and artificial moralistic limitation on my freedom that I would no longer allow to hold me back from living as I wanted. The more I thought about it, the more I felt like an impostor—and a lonely one. So many of my friendships were predicated on a shared faith that I no longer shared, and I started drifting away from many of them.

Eventually, I stopped attending any of my classes, and I was lucky if I got out of bed more than three or four days a week. I quit school and took a full-time, year-round position as a teacher in a preschool for children of migrant workers where I'd had a summer job every year for the past several years.

I drove through a canyon along the Columbia River to get to work at the preschool every day. And each day for months, the darkness had been growing in my mind. One day, I decided, *Today is the day. I'm done.* A refrain playing on repeat in my mind: *I'm done. It's over. I don't care, don't even want to care.*

All I wanted was to find out what it would feel like for my ancient hatchback to slam into the icy cold water and be carried away. *How far will it go?* I wondered idly, then shook my head. *Who cares?*

I was less than a minute away from the spot. A quarter mile past the "Port of Mattawa" sign, just below the dam. A little pull-out for scenic views meant no guardrail, no obstacles to the edge of the cliff except a few tumbleweeds. I had my seat belt off, accelerator down, and nothing to disrupt my determination.

Nothing except that face.

Suddenly he was looking at me. Not *really*, but in my mind I could see him, as clear as day, and he seemed so sad. He was wearing a crown of thorns. It looked painful, but somehow regal. He was wondering if this was really how I wanted to meet him. *Wouldn't*

we like to get to know each other first? Would you give me a chance? I
hit the brake, eased over to the side of the road, and sobbed. I had
to give him a chance.

That face . . . somehow, I thought I could look at that face forever.

I called in sick to work and an hour later found myself crying
alone in the adoration chapel at the parish. I called a friend, who
came and listened and cried with me. She set me up with a coun-
selor affiliated with our church, and I slept on her sofa for a few
nights. The adoration chapel soon became my safe place. I knew
Jesus was there. Catholics believe that Jesus is really and truly present in the host, the bread that gets consecrated at Mass. In an adoration chapel, the host is displayed for us to look at and be with.
Jesus was with me. He was real, and I had a deep need to get to
know him. Everything I had read before, everything I had learned
in Bible studies and heard in homilies and had rolled my eyes at in
cheesy art in childhood catechism classes—it was all true. But what
mattered most to me was that he *knew* me. He knew what I was
going to do that day driving along the river. He knew everything
I had done prior to that moment, and even the things I didn't yet
know I would do—and he cared.

This love was a brand-new experience for me. It was almost ad-
dictive. I spent an hour or two a day in the adoration chapel before
the Blessed Sacrament. Sometimes I would read my Bible, sometimes I'd bring paperwork to catch up on, and sometimes I'd just sit

and gaze at him, trying to wrap my head around what it meant that he loved me.

This went on for a couple of years. One day, I was sitting on the floor of the chapel barefoot, reading the Gospel of John, and I came across the line where Jesus says, "No one can come to me unless the Father who sent me draws him" (John 6:44). I realized that I had come to Jesus—here I was, sitting right in front of him. And the only reason I was able to be there was because God the Father had drawn me there. He had been drawing me my entire life to this moment here in this chapel; a moment in which he would help me to see clearly that he had been with me through everything I had ever been through, that my pain was his pain and that my joy had been his joy. And he was with me right now. I had a Father who loved me dearly. A Father who had never once chosen some intoxicating substance over his beloved daughter, who had instead given over his very Son in order to draw her closer to himself. I was floored.

I don't know how long I sat there, making prayers of gratitude and praise, tears streaming down my face. After a long silence, though, I heard Jesus whisper to my heart, "Would you consider making yourself all mine?"

"Um. What?" was my eloquent answer. The question was repeated, and then silence. I had no idea what it meant, except that maybe I was losing my mind. Was this one of those religious manic breaks that people talk about? I decided I had made it up, and that

I would definitely not ever say anything to anyone about it. In fact, I probably needed to stop spending so much time in the chapel, I decided. And I did. I only went once or twice a week over the next few months, until a friend confided in me that she was discerning her vocation.

"What does that mean?" I asked, confused.

"I'm praying about whether I might have a religious vocation."

"Okaaay . . . ? Still not getting it." I shook my head at her. "Sounds like a big deal, though. What does that look like?"

She laughed. "It means I think God might want me to be a religious sister. A nun." She shook her head. "Julie the Jesus freak doesn't know about this?"

"Do people still really do that?" I asked, ignoring the jab. I was sure my face had gone completely white. *Would you consider making yourself all mine?* This couldn't be what he'd meant, could it? No, that was crazy. Nuns are like an extinct species or something. I had never even seen one in real life! She had to be making this up.

"I mean, not around here, really. But yeah, there's a lot of young communities that are still growing." She shrugged. My reaction was making her uncomfortable. "I don't know. I think it's kind of cool."

"No! It is! It's just . . . I didn't know people still did that. Like, I didn't even know it was still even an option! And it's just . . ." I paused, unsure whether I should say what I was thinking.

"What? You don't think I should do it?"

"It's not that . . . it's just . . ." I was suddenly feeling very drawn to the idea. I didn't even know yet what it would mean, but somehow I knew that this was the invitation Jesus was extending. Whatever it was, if he wanted it, so did I. "I think maybe *I* should."

She burst out laughing. "Yeah, actually, you probably should." I told her about my experience in the chapel, and she told me about a magazine that listed hundreds of different religious communities and details about how they lived, prayed, and ministered.

I first met the Daughters of St. Paul at a national conference for Catholic young adults. Sister Tracey Dugas (whom you'll meet in another chapter) was giving a talk about using media to evangelize on campus, and in the middle of her talk she showed a short clip from *The Return of the King*. The clip paused on a close-up of Aragorn, sword drawn, hair flowing in the wind, looking regal and rugged and ready to save the day. Sister stopped, looked at the screen, and said, "I'm going to tell y'all a secret." With a conspiratorial whisper and a mischievous look in her eye, she said, "If you ever hear a nun say, 'That man could play a good Jesus,' what she means is, 'That man is a hottie.'" Then, gesturing back to the screen, she said, "And I gotta say, that man would make a good Jesus." When the laughter had finally subsided, she spoke honestly and beautifully about the special relationship she had with the Lord, and told about how she truly experienced him as a spouse. It set my heart on fire, and I wanted what she had. So, naturally, I avoided her at all costs for the rest of the conference. At the following year's conference, though, I found another Daughter of St. Paul and we had a long conversation. Patiently, she answered all my questions and asked me a few in return. Then she invited me to come to a retreat at the motherhouse in Boston over Holy Week.

I thoroughly enjoyed that visit. Sisters shared with us their way of approaching prayer and deeper reflections on the mission of evangelizing through media. Celebrating Holy Thursday, Good Friday, Holy Saturday, and Easter Sunday with the sisters was an experience like none other. I had never experienced reverence like that before; it was clear that every single person in that chapel was deeply in love with Jesus and was truly desiring to enter into the experience of accompanying him from the sorrow and pain of the Cross to the jubilation of the Resurrection.

The highlight of that retreat, though, was a particularly rowdy Easter egg hunt in which at least two different sisters were shoved into snowdrifts, snowballs had been hurled, and full-on tug-of-wars had been had over the Golden Egg—which counted for ten regular eggs. It had been utterly delightful, and I found myself spellbound by what some sisters considered inappropriate behavior. "You'll scandalize our visitors!" one sister had shouted. Ha. Scandalize? I was bent over laughing, finally convinced I wanted to be one of them.

I visited twice more, but then I fell into some old patterns and came to the conclusion that I would never be a good enough person to enter religious life. I was just too broken, too weak, and too *much*. I knew I still wanted to evangelize, though, so when an opportunity came to work in full-time youth ministry, I took it.

Nearly a decade after that first visit to the sisters, I was slicing tomatoes at my kitchen counter. I found myself praying, spontaneously offering my experiences of ministry that day as a gift to Jesus. *And what about my gift?* I heard him reply. I put down the knife, sat down at the table, and cried. I knew *exactly* what he meant. He had been trying to give me a gift—a precious invitation to be all his. I had turned him down, returned the envelope as undeliverable. Now I could feel him there, with me, gently smiling, still holding his hand out. The invitation was still there, and now I knew I needed to accept it.

I was still Facebook friends with one of the sisters I had met during my visits, so I sent her a DM and asked if we could talk. A few months later, I flew out to visit again and be interviewed as part of the application process for entering, and before I knew it, I was giving my notice at the parish I worked at and donating most of my possessions to a secondhand shop. It had been ten years, but it was also a whirlwind.

In the opening chapters of *The Hobbit*, the dwarves are convinced that Bilbo Baggins should be excluded from the adventure they have planned. He's jumpy and not nearly fierce enough, but there was a sign on the door marking him as chosen for the journey, so they are perplexed. Bilbo protests that he'd just painted his door, and there couldn't possibly be a mark. That's when the wise wizard Gandalf settles the argument, verifying that there was, in fact, a mark on the door: "I put it there myself. For very good reasons. You asked me to find the fourteenth man for your expedition, and I chose Mr. Baggins."

Jesus chose me for this life. I don't pretend to know why, and it's possible there are moments when my sisters wonder, too! But he put his mark on me. He claimed my heart, and there is nothing I or anyone else can do to revoke his claim. He continues to hold his hand out to me, each time he invites me to speak a yes that calls to a deeper place in my heart or that requires a little bigger sacrifice or just a little more trust. I still sometimes answer, "Not yet." But he's patient. He will keep inviting and guiding and carrying me until finally I get to be home with him forever. And in the end, that's what I'm living for. Without that, without heaven, my life doesn't make sense . . . and I like it that way.

ABOUT THE AUTHORS

The Daughters of Saint Paul is a Roman Catholic international religious congregation founded in 1915 in Italy. The congregation is part of the worldwide Pauline Family, one of the ten institutes founded by James Alberione, and operates in fifty-one countries around the world. Their international headquarters is based in Rome and their US headquarters is based in Boston.

Contributors:

Sr. Amanda Marie Detry, FSP, was born in Pennsylvania and grew up in Wisconsin and Arizona. She made her First Profession with the Daughters of St. Paul in June 2019. She currently lives in St. Louis, Missouri.

Sr. Tracey Dugas, FSP, is originally from south Louisiana and grew up eating gumbo, crawfish, and listening to Cajun music. She earned a master of arts in theological studies from Notre Dame Seminary in New Orleans, Louisiana. She is currently stationed in Chicago, where she serves as director of Pauline Mission Advancement. Follow Sr. Tracey's creative work on Instagram: @Sistah_Tee_Letters.

Sr. Danielle Victoria Lussier, FSP, is originally from Michigan and is now based in New York City. She is a junior professed sister, entering her eighth year as a Daughter of St. Paul.

Sr. Jacqueline Jean-Marie Gitonga, FSP, is a Daughter of St. Paul who was born and raised in Kenya, Africa. She is currently missioned in New Orleans, where, with her sisters, she joyfully lives and shares the treasures of her Catholic faith through writing, faith formation talks, retreats, and social media.

Sr. Emily Beata Marsh, FSP, is originally from Buffalo, New York. She entered the Daughters of St. Paul in 2007, and is currently stationed in Alexandria, Virginia, where she serves as national vocation director.

Sr. K. Andrew Marie Tyler, FSP, was born in Houston, Texas. Since leaving Texas to follow Jesus, she has lived in many different places and currently lives in St. Louis, Missouri.

Sr. Maria Kim-Ngân Bùi, FSP, is originally from Tempe, Arizona, and now serves as the director of marketing and sales at the sisters' publishing house in Boston. She is a writer for Blessed Is She, loves to read, sing, and to have long conversations over coffee. She lives in Boston.

Sr. Julie Marie Benedicta Turner, FSP, is a lover of coffee, puppies, and gadgets. She's a die-hard Seahawks fan, which sometimes puts her at odds with the members of her current community in Boston, where she works full-time to help get fun and beautiful Catholic books into the hands of schoolkids.

CPSIA information can be obtained
at www.ICGtesting.com
Printed in the USA
BVHW080146120522
636764BV00003B/3